Missing Max

Finding Hope After My Marine Son's Death

Advantage™
INSPIRATIONAL

Julie Burget Schrock

Proud Mother of Max and Ryan Donahue

Missing Max by Julie Burget Schrock

ISBN 13: 978-1-59755-269-1

Published by: ADVANTAGE BOOKS™, Longwood, Florida
www.advbookstore.com

The Sound of Music. Robert Wise, Twentieth Century Fox Film Corporation, Argyle Enterprises, 1965

Forrest Gump. Robert Zemeckis, Paramount, 1994.

Rocky Mountain High, By John Denver and Mike Taylor, © 1972 by RCA

If You Could See Me Now, By Kim Noblitt, (c) 1992 by Integrity's Praise/BMI and Dad and Dann Music

Amazing Grace, John Newton, 1779

Bible quotations are taken from the Women's Devotional Bible, New International Version. Copyright 1990 by The Zondervan Corporation

Hero Bracelets, www.herobracelets.org

My First Christmas in Heaven. Miscellaneous sources; attributed to Ben, a 13-year-old boy who died in 1997 of a brain tumor. He gave the poem to his mother prior to his death.

The Case for Christ; A Journalist's Personal Investigation of the Evidence for Jesus. Lee Strobel, Copyright 1998 by Zondervan

"Sorry," "Catch Phrase" and "Yahtzee" are trademarks of Hasbro Inc.

Library of Congress Control Number: 2011932662

Cover design by Pat Theriault

First Printing: July 2011
11 12 13 14 15 16 17 10 9 8 7 6 5 4 3 2 1
Printed in the United States of America

Dedication

I'm writing this book for Ryan, Max's brother, who, as of this writing, has yet to cry. I can only wonder where his pain is directed.

And for Chad, Taylor, Jordan, Judy, my family and my friends, who continue to get me through this time in my life. I love you all.

And for Max, who will forever be loved and never forgotten.

Acknowledgments

I don't know how anyone survives the death of a child without a belief that they will be together again. I also don't know how such a time can be experienced without the love, support and patience of friends and family.

My trials may seem more than experienced by most, but I feel as though the love and support that pours over me is also more than experienced by most. Even though this horrible event has happened in my life, I still feel blessed.

For their love, support and patience, I want to thank:

My husband, Chad. I love you more than you know.

Ryan, Devan, Taylor and Jordan

Judy Shine and Gary Garrison

My family

My friends

My family at Charter Financial Resources

My friends at Shine Investment Advisory Services

My friends that feel like family at "Life's Sweet"

Rhonda and Todd Saemisch

Cindy Sloan Butts, my editor

Kim Wheeler, photographer

And to all who have kept my family and me in their prayers, I am forever grateful.

This experience has introduced me to extraordinary people performing selfless acts of kindness for families such as mine. They use their talents to send families of fallen soldiers a portrait of their loved one and they do so at their own expense. The portraits of Max provide a comfort and peace that I did not think I could experience.

Please take a moment to visit their websites and consider sending your thanks.

The Michael G. Reagan Portrait Foundation
www.fallenheroesproject.org

Kaziah Hancock and Project Compassion
www.kaziahthegoatwoman.com

Section I

MAX

August 4, 2010 – My nightmare begins

"Honey, you know I love you very much, right?"

"Yes, what's happened -- Is Max okay?"

"Honey, I love you very much."

"WHERE IS MAX, IS HE ALIVE?"

So began the nightmare that has become my new life; the sweetest of words as a preface to the most personal of tragedies.

It was Wednesday, August 4, 2010. I was in Michigan, driving to my sister Kris's house with my other sister, Polly, and my mother, when I got the phone call. Earlier that morning at our home in Denver, my husband Chad opened the door to the sight feared more than any other -- two Marines standing on the doorstep. My son, Max, was a Marine Corporal serving as a working dog handler, currently deployed in Afghanistan.

Chad was told that Max had been hit by an IED (Improvised Explosive Device). As a result, both his legs and his right arm had been amputated. He was alive and they were trying to get him out of Afghanistan and into Germany. Once stabilized, he would be flown to Bethesda, Maryland, where his treatment would begin. As bad as the situation sounded, the "good" news was that Max was alive.

My sister pulled the car over, Mom and I got out, and we held each other, screaming and crying, my knees buckling under me. These were the cries that no mother should have to hear and no mother should have to cry. I had never made such sounds in my life. Anyone watching would have witnessed the breaking of two mothers' hearts.

There was another two-hour grueling car ride ahead of us until I could arrive at Kris's house and begin planning whatever way possible to get back to Denver. All I could think of was that I had to get to Max. I did not want my son going through this alone. Praying that he was so sedated he would have no memory of the pain his body was suffering, I asked God over and over for Max to get the attention he needed in order to make it home. All I could think was, "Just get him to me and I'll take it from there. Please!"

My brother Bill and his wife Debbie were also on their way to Kris's. Bill's daughter Jenny had once worked in a VA hospital, in the rehabilitation unit. She immediately started e-mailing articles about other amputees who were living full lives. Jenny assured me that even though Max's legs were amputated above the knee, he could still be fitted with prosthetics. His arm was amputated below the elbow, so I knew he could be fitted with a very workable prosthetic, but I had not been sure about his legs. It was good news for me, as his mother, but I knew that it would take months for Max to be ready mentally to confront the loss of the body for which he had so much pride.

I remember hating the state of Michigan (sorry Michiganders), because the vacation spot of my youth was the place where I experienced the death or injury of those I loved most. Several years earlier, the boys, (Max and Ryan), my mom, dad, brother and I were in a very bad car accident.

My dad was driving and, as we were coming down a hill, the car hydroplaned, hit, then flipped on top of a guard rail, did two revolutions in the air, and landed upside down at the bottom of a hill. My dad was killed almost instantly. Everyone else crawled out of the car and walked up the hill in a manner reminiscent of the Von Trapp family walking single file, up a mountain. My dad's death took place in Michigan and now, while in Michigan, I was getting the news of Max's injuries.

What a blessing to me that I wasn't at home that morning to open the door and see the two Marines. It was my worst nightmare and a vision that I had learned to roll up and kick out of my head as soon as it entered. I was spared that experience, but Chad wasn't.

Spreading the Word

Those first few minutes and hours continue to be unimaginable to me. But, if they were hard for me to believe, what were they to Chad? Both our lives changed the moment that he opened the door and saw the Marines standing there. Chad was made the messenger of news that would utterly break his wife's heart, at the same time that his heart was breaking. How do you deliver that type of news? What words do you use? When do you make the call? What about Ryan (Max's brother) and Taylor (step-brother)?

Chad had plans to meet a friend for coffee that morning. As Chad is never late, Gary called to see what was holding him up. Gary is also the husband of Judy, my best friend since the eighth grade.

Judy is not only my best friend, but she has been Max and Ryan's acting Aunt since their birth. Every Christmas, Thanksgiving and almost all birthdays have been shared with Judy and her family. She is and always has been an integral part of the boys' and my life. Judy and I have shared our teen years, college, marriage, babies, divorce, deaths, all our life's experiences, but this would be our biggest trial together. Add her name to Chad's list of "how do I tell?" As it turned out, Chad didn't have to make that call to Judy because she was getting the message second-hand through Gary's reactions to his conversation with Chad.

Gary -- "Chad, where are you? …. Oh no, [expletive."]

Judy -- "Is it Max?"

Gary -- "Yes. He's been hurt really bad, but he's alive."

Judy recalls thinking immediately that Max would be okay; that his condition was bad but he would live through it. We would all pull together and work out whatever Max needed. She didn't let herself think that there was a possibility he would not make it.

I wanted Judy to go with Chad to tell Ryan, but Chad elected to go alone. Other than Max not getting hurt in the first place, this is one situation that I wish had been different. I wish I had been there for Ryan.

The rest of that day, Ryan and Chad were together -- later to be joined by Taylor who was attending summer session at the University of Colorado in Boulder. I was able to get home to Denver by 8:00 the night of August 4, 2010, and was met by Chad, Ryan and Taylor. It was good to be "home" but "home" would never be the same, for any of us.

My Max

Before continuing, I'd like to, in a way, introduce you to Max.

He was born on July 14, 1987. Max wasn't due for another two weeks so, thinking we had plenty of time before his birth, my then-husband Greg, went out of state on a business trip. There was a 24-hour period of time when Greg and my best friend Judy would both be out of town. Yes, that's when Max decided that he was ready to arrive. So, at 3:00 in the morning, I'm watching the clock to allow enough time to drive myself to the hospital between contractions.

As my labor lasted 24 hours, Judy made it back in time for the first shift and Greg made it back for the delivery -- three epidurals later! Max got stuck and had to be suctioned out. It was my first clue of what was to come. He rarely did anything the conventional way.

All mothers feel, or should feel, that their child is special -- but Max really was! He was absolutely beautiful, each day of his 23 years. This was not a fact that was hidden from the boy -- he knew it. I used to love to walk behind him, to watch the reactions of the young girls. It was quite a study of mating and dating rituals and I never tired of watching people watching him.

Max was protective and stood up for those who couldn't or wouldn't defend themselves. He loved stepping in and correcting what he defined as an injustice. He fought -- verbally, mentally and physically -- the inequalities people set upon each other. He was his own equalizer. If he thought something wasn't right, he would step in to correct it.

The principal at his high school, Mr. Morgan, told this story of Max and it was read at his funeral.

My first week on the job at DC Oakes, Max came busting into my office needing Mr. Simons and me to follow him over to Safeway. He wanted both of us to help him rough up a guy who was hassling a couple of our girls...hilarious...asking the principal and a teacher to help him take care of some shady character in a nearby parking lot! I tell that story all the time... it reminds me of Max's protective nature. He cared so much for the people around him.

I'm not suggesting that this behavior is right for everyone. Imagine the society, high school or home where each member acted out his or her own version of vigilante justice. But, in a world now where so few do, so few step in, and most choose to watch a crime instead of stop one, it was reassuring to know that Max was present.

Growing up, Max did get into trouble, in and outside of our home. And to those who would say he wasn't so great or that he was a troublemaker, I would ask them, "Have you ever paid for a stranger's full tank of gas when their credit card was declined? Have you ever refused money for helping an older couple when their car broke down? When was the last time you stopped and helped someone whose car slid off the road? When was the last time you put yourself in harm's way to protect someone else?"

Max did all these and more. He made it a point to do numerous acts of kindness.

I may sound defensive, and I know that Max was no angel on this earth, but I know with all my heart that he is one now.

Max was a larger-than-life type of person. He never entered a room quietly (unless he was prowling in preparation for a pounce on his brother). At his funeral, one of his high school teachers wrote of Max's strength and physical presence. Mr. Talbert wrote:

Right before his last deployment, Max was kind enough to give us a visit. All of a sudden, this big shadow appeared above my head. He shook my hand...my knuckles coming together in a knot. He slapped me on the back...my teeth almost popping out. I told him, "Take it easy on me...I'm old." That's what I remember about Max...a wonderful kid who was friendly 'til it hurt.

Max and his brother Ryan were as close as two brothers could be. They grew up tossing each other around; our household was no stranger to blood and bruises. But when Max came back from boot camp -- his muscles "ripped" and ready to show off his new "skills" -- Ryan knew he stood little chance of getting the best of him. Ryan's only defense was his ability to outrun Max, which he proved on many occasions!

I'll never forget getting the boys together for our Christmas card picture and Ryan walking in with a black eye. The story they told me was that the boys were wrestling and Max's elbow met with Ryan's eye. Over a year passed before Ryan told me that he blackened his own eye. "Max was going to do it so I did it myself before he could." In Ryan's mind, he had won that one. I still don't understand that "logic!"

Max was a wonderful son and devoted brother. It is impossible to believe that he is gone and that all we have left of him are our memories.

Max the Marine

You might be wondering why Max wanted to become a Marine in the first place.

Only he could answer that, but I think I know when he first got the idea: September 11, 2001. Max and I had a conversation shortly after the attack on the twin towers. He was 14 years old, in the 8th grade, when he said, "Mom, when I'm old enough, I am going to sign up to fight."

I replied, "Honey, as an American woman, that fills me with pride, but as your mother, it scares me to death."

It has been a long time since I've thought about that conversation with Max. Looking back now, as we were in the midst of those horrific days after 9/11, I had no way to realize the significance that those events would have on my life. I had no way to know that Max would follow through with his desire to "sign up and fight."

Five days after Max's 19th birthday, he entered the Marine Corps. Chad and I dropped him off at the recruiting station. After hard hugs were given and good-byes were spoken, he walked toward the recruiting center door. I can still see him turning to us, waving and smiling as he entered.

There are no words to describe the intensity of the sadness and fear that I felt -- truly, no words. When Max joined the Marine Corps, we all joined and, like it or not, I was now the mother of a Marine. And I did not like it at all.

Boot camp turned out to be everything that I had heard it would be -- horrible. The only good thing about those thirteen weeks was the letters that I received from Max, and he wrote a lot of letters. The boy was miserable. As a result, I was miserable!

We flew to San Diego for his boot camp graduation. The first time I saw him, I acted like a teenage groupie, screaming his name and waving. When the units were released from graduation, I was finally allowed to hold him. I felt thirteen weeks of angst and emotional wear-and-tear physically released from me.

I have heard it said that being a Marine changes a person. Although his voice seemed deeper and his body was definitely more muscular, I did not notice any major changes. To me, Max was a respectful, loving young man when he entered the Marine Corps and that had not changed.

One thing that did change was his body. He worked at perfecting the manly V-shape to his back and the rolling, hill-like biceps that he used as the canvas for his many tattoos. What he didn't have to perfect, as it came naturally to him, was the squinty-eyed smile that became his trademark. It is the feature mentioned most when people recall him, that and his powerful physical presence.

The events of August 4 continue

Angel on the Plane

When my brother and his wife dropped me off at the Detroit airport, I remember thinking, "Whatever is going to come, take it one step at a time, beginning with getting to Denver." I was very angry and very anxious. The thought of a plane trip surrounded by people in a close, confined space was mortifying. My only consolation was that I had a window seat in a two-seat row.

Enter the man whom I now call my angel. When he sat down, I thought, "This poor man is in for a miserable flight -- sitting next to a worried, grieving mother." I didn't realize it then, but it's very clear to me now -- God sent this man to me. I mean that with all my heart. Within the first three minutes, he heard what was happening -- my son - Marine - Afghanistan - lost both legs and right arm - have to get him out of Afghanistan to Germany - then Bethesda ....

Before I tell you how he responded, consider those moments. What would you do, say, think or feel? I don't have that answer for myself but I now have a good blueprint to follow.

This man/angel from Scotland with his lovely accent spent the entire plane ride from Detroit to Denver, consoling me -- holding my hand -- crying with me -- and at one precious point, when our conversation lulled and I started quietly crying, he pulled me into his arms and held me while I wept. I will never forget him telling me that America is the country that steps in to protect the world and that other countries should be grateful. I appreciated hearing that. I couldn't bear the thought of what was happening to Max to be in vain.

I continue to marvel at God's greatness and his capacity to care for us. I believe this wonderful man (whose name I don't know and don't need to remember) was sent by heaven to get me from Detroit to Denver. There, the arms and love of my husband, son, stepson and best friend were waiting to hold me and start getting me through the horror that would redefine my life. But until I made it to Denver, God sent an angel to help me through the flight.

As I de-planed I said, "I'll never forget you." He replied, "Nor I you" and that was it. I've never seen or heard from him again, but will never forget his kindness and his role in what remain as the worst moments in my life.

A New Life for Max

First thing Thursday morning, Judy was at the door. At that point, they were still trying to get Max out of Afghanistan into Germany. I wasn't sure who "they" were but was told that they would stabilize him in Germany, enough to get him to Bethesda. That's where I would finally be with him and start the grueling process of having his medical needs addressed while planning his rehabilitation. I can remember saying, "Bethesda is the goal -- just get him to Bethesda."

As there was little word on his condition or location, Judy started leading me through "the plan." She had clients with a townhome in Bethesda where she was sure I could stay when the government-paid housing was exhausted.

Judy -- "He's going to be in rehab at least nine, maybe twelve months. So you'll be living in Bethesda for most of the next year."

Judy continued with the rationalization that gave me the greatest amount of hope.

"It's a good sign that they amputated -- that means he's healthy enough to have a chance of making it."

If there were no hope, why would they go to the trouble of amputating? I had a real sense that Max would make it, at least to Bethesda, where I would be able to see and hold him.

I still didn't know anything about the condition of Max's head but was sure that he was being heavily sedated, which gave me a modicum of peace. I did not want him to remember any of the pain his body was experiencing, nor did I want him to be afraid or feel alone.

That afternoon, Ryan, Taylor and I went for a hike near Franktown, Colorado, to get away from the house for a while. Colorado is such a wonderful state; Ryan took us to the part of a trail that had an exceptionally beautiful view. It was on that hike that I gave Ryan and Taylor their "marching orders" (that Judy had previously given to me).

"Max's life will be different but full. He can still have children and live life and, in time, he'll walk with the help of prosthetics. It will be up to you guys to keep his mind in the game. It will be important for you and Max's peers to continue to include him…."

That was Max's situation and I was dedicated to it. We would just need time for him to work on his rehab and get used to the prosthetics. I knew it would be a long road, but the final destination was hopeful and do-able and positive.

We get the call

Later that evening, the end of day two, we had little news. Max was still in Afghanistan -- they had tried to fly out but had to turn around. No explanation was offered as to why, but it wasn't difficult to deduce -- it was Afghanistan, after all. We had little word on his medical condition and the information that we were receiving wasn't good. I can remember asking, "What about his mind -- is there any damage to his brain?"

The response ripped at my heart. "There's still no word Ma'am -- is your passport in order?"

It was then that I became unhinged. "You can't call with no news on his medical condition and ask if my passport is in order. I need to talk to a doctor. How can I talk to his doctor?"

Chad grabbed the phone and tried to get information but he became angry as well -- loudly saying a word that rarely, if ever, comes out of my sweet husband's mouth. Things were not so heated that I didn't instinctively reprimand his cursing!

I think that it was during that phone call when we realized Bethesda was an optimistic and unlikely goal. We hung up, expecting to get word from a doctor in the early hours of the next morning, Friday August 6, 2010.

The phone rang at approximately 4:30am. Max was brain dead. My 23 year-old son was no longer alive. The pain was and is excruciating, even as I write this months later.

We were asked permission for his organs to be donated. Max had previously signed his intent for organ donation, but they preferred to get permission from the parents as well. In order to donate his organs, he would need to be kept on life support for the next day or so. That's why there is some confusion regarding his date of death. In some places it is recorded as August 6, in others as August 7. For me, it's August 6.

Telling the brothers

Taylor spent the night at Ryan's house, so Chad and I left the house at 6:00 am, to drive out and tell them. On the way, we went through the fast food lane to get coffee. I realized at the window that this was the location of Max's first paycheck job. Max worked as the order taker at that very window. Ryan used to sit on the grass across from the window and wait for him to have a break or finish working. I could picture them both, Max working and Ryan waiting. The boys were always so very close; how would I find the words to tell Ryan his brother was gone?

As we drove to Ryan's house Chad said:

"Can I tell you something? Did you feel me jolt in bed this morning?"

"No."

"Honey, I have to tell you what happened. While I was sleeping I saw Max's face, eyes staring me straight in the eye with that big smile on his face --you know the smile, the really big one. It was so vivid, so real. He was just looking at me with that big smile. I remember that I opened my eyes and looked to see what time it was. I felt like he was saying good-bye and letting me know he was okay."

I got an immense measure of peace from that. It surprised me that I was also a little envious. I wanted to see Max's smile again. Chad said it probably would have been too much for me to see and his appearing to Chad was Max's way of getting the message to me as well. Still, I find myself closing my eyes and waiting for my "visit." I hear other "gold star" parents (parents of military children that have died) tell of their "visits." I'm still hoping for mine.

As odd as it seems, telling Ryan, Devan (Ryan's fiancé), and Taylor that Max was gone seemed almost unemotional. No one screamed or broke down in tears; the news was accepted quietly and without questions. We were all in shock. Chad and I stayed only a few minutes as what more was there to do or say, at this moment anyway? There would be a lot to say later. But right now we all needed time to process.

The realization hit me that all my "eggs" were now in one basket, Ryan's. It was and still is a VERY vulnerable feeling. What if I lost Ryan? What if I outlived both my sons? I know that it can happen. All you need to do is walk through a cemetery and read the headstones to see the evidence; headstones of siblings with the same date of death. Or brother and sister buried next to each other, with dates of death only a few years apart. Horrible, heart-breaking headstones.

I'll spend the rest of my days hovering over Ryan, I'm sure. At least in my heart. He would never tolerate the intrusiveness of a true "helicopter" mom. I give his safety and well-being up to God in prayer each morning. I have also received Ryan's assurance that he, too, has given his life to the Lord. Heaven holds a greater hope for me now than it ever did before. It is the only place and time where we will all be together again.

Taylor, his step-brother

My poor stepson Taylor was watching and absorbing all of these events as they unfolded -- I can't imagine what was going through his mind. He seemed calm, but his facial expressions twisted with worry. It was all so bewildering and unreal.

I have since asked Taylor his recollection of those days. He wrote the following:

Up until August 4th, 2010, I have never had to deal with anything as emotionally drowning. When the news first came in, I was devastated. I was in disbelief that anything could have happened to Max, of all people.

Directly after my Dad called me, I went for a long run -- a natural escape for me. Normally my runs are mentally clear and free, but this run clearly was far from ordinary. The entire run, my body felt numb. When normally I only run 4 miles, that morning I ran 10. I was filled with worry.

I was trying to place myself in Max's position, although clearly it was impossible. I was trying to imagine what he was going through, even to the point where I felt a weird physical tingling sensation in my legs and right arm, knowing Max had his amputated. I cried and cried in the shower, and the entire drive down to the house. I was terrified for you, too. I didn't know what you were going through, being that you were in Michigan, and I was afraid to call you because I didn't know what to say.

I was also worried for Ryan's sake. I wasn't sure how he was handling the situation either. All I knew was that I had to hold it together for you and Ryan and be as strong a support as I could. As I was waiting for Ryan to arrive, I stared out into the gulch with a gut-wrenching feeling. I was expecting the worse upon his arrival. I was very nervous to see him.

Throughout the rest of the day, the thoughts that consumed me were of wanting to help Max. Being that I am resourceful in nature, I thought there was somehow, some way that I could. Being that I couldn't, I was even further distraught. With my physiology studies and background, I thought a lot about what his body was internally going through. I don't know why I thought this but I was trying to figure out how his body was handling the situation and the mechanisms as to how he was going to make it through the trauma.

The next couple of days are pretty blurry in my memory. I remember feeling an innate need to be at Ryan's side as much as possible. We consoled each other but we didn't talk about the situation much except once, when we were alone at Ryan's kitchen table. Our feelings started to pour out, Ryan's at a level of anger I have not witnessed previously, and my feeling an extreme intensity of fear for what Max's life would be like, or even worse, that he wouldn't make it.

I remember standing at the counter when my Dad was on the phone with Garrett. We started to learn about further injury Max sustained that we were previously unaware of. Witnessing you hearing the news as a bystander was a deepening level of pain. Mentally, I thought I had lost it. My face dropped and I felt like I had seized, as if I could no longer process. My mind went numb with everything I was feeling.

It was worse than rubbing salt in a wound. I was filled with even more disbelief. I didn't want to believe what was going on and that Max fell victim. At this time I didn't even want to look outside, I didn't want to see anyone walking down the sidewalk, I didn't want to see any outsiders. I was aggravated by the fact of how little we did know at the time, or what they would/would not share with us.

Being as hopeful as I was, I was thinking a lot about how Max's life was going to be changed if he made it through. I thought about all the fun things we were still going to do with him, but at the same time fearful of how Max would have handled the situation psychologically. All I wanted was for everything to be okay.

I think that it's healing for Taylor to be able to put his feelings into words; it's comforting for him, and for me. Up to this point, Ryan has been unable to do so. I worry.

Judy, my best friend

As I said before, Judy and I have been best friends since junior high school. Her grief over Max, I am sure, is only slightly less than mine. The day that Max died, she immediately went into action. Judy asked Rhonda (who works for her) to create a website for Max so that we would have a place to communicate to family and friends without making multiple calls. Judy and Gary found the cemetery, Judy bought my black dress for the funeral and she was there to help me pick out Max's burial plot. With all she did and does, she's never made me feel as though I was pushing the limits on our friendship. Sharing the experience of losing Max has brought us even closer.

Judy has since said that she worries about my "throwing in the towel." She was concerned that my divorce, cancer (I had breast cancer in 2008, all is well, get those mammograms!), the car accident that killed Dad, and now Max's death, would be more than I could handle and that I would mentally "check out." I assured her that this was not and would not be the case. What kind of testament to my faith, or to Max, would that be if I gave up? I either trust in God or I don't. And, as it turns out, I do. Also, I would never do that to Ryan, Chad, my family or to my best friend.

Immediately after hearing that Max had died, I temporarily removed all my pictures of him from the house. It was too painful for me to look at him. Judy's response was the opposite. She pulled out pictures of Max and spread them on her dining room table. She immersed herself in Max, not willing or ready to start thinking of him as a memory. I believe that she was trying to keep him alive for as long as she could.

I am continually touched by Judy's love for my boys, Max and Ryan (and Taylor and Jordan). I am continually amazed at her love for me.

Note -- Judy and Gary have decided to be buried in the same cemetery as Max.

My "Lieutenant Dan" Wish

The two days before Max died, I can remember thinking a lot about the movie *Forrest Gump*. I clung to the vision of Lieutenant Dan walking toward Forrest on the day of his wedding. It was the scene where Lieutenant Dan had his "new" legs, new life and new fiancé. That would be Max one day; it would just take time. Or so I hoped.

After Max died, I watched the movie again and was struck by the dialogue between Forrest and his mother on her death bed. I'm paraphrasing, but it went something like:

Why you dying Momma? (Coincidentally, Max called me *Momma*).

It's my time. Death is just a part of life; something we're all destined to do.

What's my destiny, Momma?

I don't know, Forrest. You have to figure that out on your own.

Although not ending as Max expected, I believe he did live out his own destiny. He did not have to join the Marines. It was his choice (it certainly wasn't mine). He did not have to go on this deployment; he chose to go. Apparently, he was destined to go.

I smiled when I realized that the two strongest sources of my hope came from the Bible and *Forrest Gump*!

Note -- Ryan's two dogs are named Forrest and Jenny (the names of the two main characters in the movie *Forrest Gump*). They were named months before Max died.

Broken Promise -- The last time I saw Max

Max's last visit with us was in May of 2010. He was set to deploy the following month on June 4. I was fortunate enough to have one more Mother's Day with both of my sons.

Max, Ryan and Taylor flew back to Kentucky to spend a few days with Greg (Max and Ryan's father). Their flight returned at midnight on a Tuesday. Chad and I went to pick up Ryan and Taylor. Max's flight didn't leave for several hours thereafter, so we spent some time together. After a while, Max walked Ryan and me to the car. It was the last time I saw my son. It was the last time I heard his voice or saw his walk. It was the last time I held him. As we hugged our good-byes, I couldn't keep from crying. He said:

"Don't worry, Momma, I'm going to be okay. I'm going to be back, I promise."

I said, "Do you promise?"

"Yes, I promise I'll be back."

I didn't want to let go of him. When I did get in the car, I remember looking at him through the rear view mirror as we drove away. The image is still clear -- his strong body, the way he walked, getting farther away from us. I was crying and Ryan said, "Don't worry Mom, he'll be back."

I believed him, I believed them both. But, if I'm truly honest with myself, there seemed to be a dark cloud or menacing presence hanging over us. I even ran through a red light on the way home (thank goodness it was 1:00 in the morning!). Things didn't feel right. I was just too sad. Now I think I know why. Some promises simply can't be kept.

August 4, 2010 -- Max's "last" day

Max could not have known that whatever he had for breakfast on August 4, 2010, would be his last. He had no way of knowing that everything he did that day would be "his last." None of us did and none of us do. I believe that's a good thing.

When my mind goes to what his last few moments might have been like, it shakes me to my core. I physically react to the thought of his body being blown apart. When the thought creeps into my mind, my eyes well up with tears and I feel nauseous. All I want to do is go home and crawl into bed.

If I could have just been there to hold him, to let him know he wasn't alone. I HATE the idea of his feeling alone, his being so far from family, as he was in those last few moments. I know his wounds were severe, severe enough to take his legs and arm. I just hope his mind was gone as well. Let his last thoughts be of life and not of death. I pray with all my heart that he never knew what hit him.

Support from across the street and around the world

It started with then California Governor Arnold Schwarzenegger lowering the flags at the state capitol to half-staff in honor of "a courageous and strong Marine." Mike Coffman, Colorado District 6 Representative, read a letter on the floor of Congress. His buddies in Afghanistan sent a video of the memorial held at Camp Leatherneck. We've been told that there is to be a K-9 kennel named after Max at Camp Pendleton. Max's name has been added to the Highland's Ranch Veterans

Memorial and the Veteran's Memorial at Cedar Hill Cemetery. A wonderful pictorial tribute was displayed at our church in Max's honor. And a tribute to him has been created at his high school, D.C Oakes in Castle Rock.

We've received over 900 letters from around the world, including General Petraus, Arnold Schwarzenegger, and President Obama. At last count, Max's website had over 90,000 hits from forty-five countries. It has been an indescribable, overwhelming experience; each letter, tribute and sympathy expressed has deepened my understanding of what it means to be an American. I came to understand that I was not going through this alone.

My neighbor bought yard flags and put them in each lawn, up and down our street. I was grateful for such a visible show of sympathy from my neighbors.

As touching as the recognition was, I was glad when things started to settle down. This was not a stage in which you want to be the center. Everything that was occurring in Max's honor was overwhelming me.

The many expressions of sympathy we received is one reason why I felt compelled to write this book. What was all "this" about? Who are the people behind the letters and the website "hits?" How do they know Max? Why do they care so much? Not having the answers made me feel as though, as close as we were, there was a part of Max that I didn't know. His family were not the only ones that loved and cared about him. Not by a long shot!

The coffin

Max wanted to be cremated, or I should say, in the event he died, Max wanted to be cremated. At this point, I was grateful that we had discussed his wishes. How awful it would have been to have had to guess what his choice would be.

In my kitchen, we were reviewing miscellaneous paperwork with Garrett (our CACO -- Casualty Assistance Calls Officer). Max had assigned all the decision-making responsibilities to me. As Garrett passed the "coffin option" pictures toward me, I gently passed them back and began to cry. "Max assigned you as his Personal Administrator," Garrett said, with sorrow pouring out of his eyes.

That moment was a turning point for me. Max had named me his Personal Administrator and I did not want him to regret that decision. I wanted him to be as proud of me as I was of him. He would not have been proud of my falling apart or being unable to cope.

I reached for the pictures and made my choice.

The funeral week

It was Wednesday, August 11, and we still didn't know exactly when Max's body would arrive in Denver. Paperwork needed to be completed in Dover, Delaware, before they could release him. Greg had arrived the previous Saturday. We had decided to have the church funeral on Friday, even if the body wasn't in Denver yet. Too many people were from out of town. As it turned out, Garrett phoned with the first piece of "good" news. Max's body was going to arrive in Denver the next day, Thursday, August 12.

The Marines' reputation for taking care of "family" is well-deserved. The respect and honor shown to my son and our family was more moving than I can yet describe. We were asked to select one of Max's Marine friends to be flown to Dover and accompany his body during the trip back to Denver. Two of Max's very close buddies are Corporals Karim Rafghi and Brett Yamashita (Yoshi).

Earlier that week, I had received a message from Karim saying that he was going to come see the family to "keep his promise to Max." I asked what that promise was. He said they had agreed that if anything happened to either of them, the other would get to the family.

Karim was in the midst of K-9 training and was not going to be permitted leave to attend Max's funeral. Yoshi was granted leave and flew to Dover to fly home with Max. The Marines simply don't leave a brother alone and I will be forever grateful for that tradition. As it turned out, Karim was able to attend the funeral.

We were introduced to a wonderful group of motorcycle-riding Americans known as the Patriot Guard. With their flags waving, they accompanied the hearse from the airport to the mortuary. As I understand, their primary purpose is to block the family from any protestors who may appear at military funerals.

Because Max's death had received extensive news coverage and knowing Max's brothers, cousins, and friends would not sit quietly while protestors shouted, we thought it a good idea to have the Patriot Guard accompany us, just in case. I grew to have great affection for these men and women who have served and experienced wartime losses.

Chad and I, Ryan and Devan, stepbrothers Jordan and Taylor, Greg and Barb (his girlfriend) and Garrett were there to meet the plane. I had to catch my breath when I first saw Yoshi stepping off. And then I caught sight of the casket, his dog tags on the handle, containing what was left of my handsome, strong, darling son's body.

The sound of the plane's engine whirling was the only sound to be heard. Anyone who was fortunate enough to be a witness was standing with salutes or hands over hearts as the casket was lowered from the plane.

The six young Marines dressed impeccably in their "blues" slowly saluted in unison, the first of many times I would see that salute during the next two days. The family slowly approached the coffin in the hearse, to greet our son and brother for the first time. I was relieved that he was finally home.

My family arrives

My family began to arrive on Wednesday, August 11. I saw them all for the first time on Thursday morning, in the hotel restaurant where they were having breakfast. My mom, brother, sisters, in-laws, nieces and nephews were all there. As I was going around the table giving hugs, I went to embrace a woman and realized I didn't know her. Who was this woman that was sharing in the gathering for my son's funeral? It turned out to be the waitress who, upon becoming familiar with my family, decided to join us. That is so like my family. No-one is a stranger and everyone is invited.

Between the tears, laughter and coffee, the large screen television flashed a picture of Max as the news reported the loss of a local Marine. I felt as though I was having an out-of-body experience; sitting with my family in a restaurant while watching my son's death reported on the television. Was this really happening? There I was, surrounded by loved ones, watching the news report the death of my first born. He was so handsome, so strong, so loved and so gone. Max would never drink coffee or laugh with us again. I knew then that it was going to be a VERY long week.

Max and his dog Ronni at Kaneohe Bay in Hawaii. This picture was on the bulletin used for his funeral.

The funeral

August 13, 2010, was a beautiful, bright, sunny Colorado day. At 12:00, three limousines arrived at the house. It was happening. There were no more decisions or plans to be made. All the events of the last nine days led to this point. And now, it was here. It was time.

As we pulled up to the chapel, I was shocked to see the number of people who lined the street, hands over hearts, saluting, flags waving. Sitting by the walkway were several German Shepherd dogs, ex-Vietnam War service dogs. Max would have liked that.

We were scooted downstairs where family members and close friends were waiting. Too many people were present and I didn't know what to do. I started to panic so Garrett found a small room by the elevator shaft and we retreated there. It was in that room where I was given Max's dog tags, the second vision I feared and had learned to block when it entered my mind. I now know that it was Gunny Smit, whom we would meet later at Camp Pendleton, who gave me the tags. At the time, I don't think that I even looked at his face.

With Garrett on my right, Chad on my left, Ryan, Devan and family members close behind, we started up the stairs. The doors opened, I saw the flag draped coffin and heard John Denver's *Rocky Mountain High*, which was so terrifically appropriate.

I would later find out that there were so many people that the chapel and balcony were filled to capacity. The overflow was sent to a separate room to watch on a live-stream screen. Because there wasn't enough room in the overflow, people were standing along the walls and out the doors. It is estimated that over 750 people were in attendance.

Chad, Taylor and I had written good-bye letters to Max, as did his father. Ryan could not bring himself to write goodbye to his brother. He wasn't ready. Our letters were read by Steffan Tubbs, a local radio personality on KOA Radio in Denver.

A word about Steffan: I listen to his radio program, almost every morning. Years earlier, Steffan had gone to Iraq to report firsthand on the war. It was during this time that Max was talking to us about wanting to join the Marine Corps.

One morning, I got into my car and turned on the radio program. Steffan was reporting that the soldier assigned to him while he was in Iraq had been killed. I could physically feel my stomach tighten. This actually occurs. People that you know, or feel that you know, are killed. This could be Max. It happens. It was happening to this soldier's family.

I could not have known then about the role Steffan would ultimately play in our lives. At the funeral, I heard his voice reading our letters and was grateful he has such a heart for the military and military families. The control of emotions that it would have required for one of my family members to read our letters would have been unfair to ask. For that matter, it was difficult for Steffan to get through some parts. I will be forever grateful to him.

Our letters read:

From: Taylor, his step-brother

Max, or Maxipad I should say…you are a one-of-a-kind man, the man who would do anything for anyone. You were the man that a person always wanted by your side in the good times and the bad; the man who would go out of his way to ensure others' happiness. You never hesitated to help someone in need, and did so selflessly. Additionally, each and every one of your friends and family members means so much to you, and you showed that on a daily basis.

You were another brother to me, like I knew from birth. While technically you were my "step brother," I never thought of you that way. In fact, I couldn't wait until I turned eighteen so I could get a tattoo with all my brothers' initials, yours included. Your presence simply brought happiness and quick smiles to our faces.

I'll never forget your blunt humor, your outgoing personality, your wish for happiness and desire to have a good time. We have had countless good times together that I will never forget. Your constant positive influence in my life will also forever shine through me.

Although you downplayed the fact you were a Marine, Ryan and I were always so proud to say, "Yeah, that's my brother, he's a Marine," even if it was to the clerk at Walmart. I am so proud of you, I'm so honored to have known you and I know I'll see you again some day.

Love, your brother Taylor

From: Chad, his stepfather

Max,

I came to love you as my own, watching you grow up over the years. I have to say without hesitation, further, that you grew into the full package as an adult man. You are handsome, fit in body and mind, respectful, intelligent, spiritual, very thoughtful of others, loving, faithful and you always had fun.

Ah...fun loving. I remember snippets like when you shoveled snow on the back porch during a heavy snow storm with your shirt off, while wearing some goofy hat with ear flaps. And times (more than once) when you wrestled on the front lawn with your brother, Ryan, at which point someone always seemed to get up bleeding somewhere, but you always got up smiling broadly.

It is that very broad bright smile I will remember first followed by thoughts and reflections of the excellent young man you grew to be. I will close with.....I love you, Max.

From: Julie, his mother

Maxie,

I always thought Ryan and I knew you best. Growing up we were such a tight little unit. You always took care of us and were so very protective. With all that's happened this past week, I've realized I was wrong. There are many, many others who knew you well. And many, many others that you took care of and protected.

I knew you as the young man who, along with your brother, paid for an older man's gas when his credit card was declined. I knew you as the man who, along with your brother and step brother, pushed an elderly couple's car to the gas station when it broke down. I can still see you declining his attempt to pay you and his blowing kisses to the car as we drove away. Ryan and I talked about it later and Ryan said, "Mom, he does that stuff all the time."

What I didn't know and have been finding out this past week is what you did for others. I've gotten so many messages with sweet stories about you. There's one in particular that paints your picture. Lisa Frey, wife of Lieutenant Colonel Grant Frey wrote:

.... I met him a few times and was always impressed with his demeanor, not to mention his smile! Until my husband reminded me, I had forgotten that Max had taken the lead in the care of our dog, Art, when we were off island to attend our daughter's K9 school graduation. When we returned after a week, Art was groomed, happy and obviously well cared for – and I had Max to thank for going above and beyond just housing him at the kennel. He spent time with Art and played with him so Art wouldn't be lonely. Because he refused to allow us to pay him, I insisted Grant take gift cards to Max and the other Marine who helped with Art. Max wanted to refuse the gift card... and had to be "ordered" to accept it. You raised a fine young man.

I spent the past weekend at Camp Lejeune with a number of Max's K9 friends. I heard many stories about Max's escapades... and if you have any doubt in your mind, I hope this eases it some. Max touched many lives and had tremendous impact on the Marines I was speaking with. Your son was loved and respected by them – love and respect that is earned, and not earned easily. He will NEVER be forgotten by any of them and our world is greatly diminished by his loss.

Maxie, what gives me my greatest peace is the conversation we had when we drove to Lookout Mountain before you left for Iraq.

I said, "Honey, I've never pushed my faith on you but I am going to now, I have to know -- Is Jesus Christ your Lord and Savior?"

"Yes, Mom, I told you that before."

"I need to hear you say it again."

And you did -- you said: "Jesus Christ is my Lord and Savior."

I said, "Okay then, you can go," (meaning to Iraq).

I know we'll be together again, honey, I truly do. It will be a long rest of my life without you, but I'll trade it for eternity with you.

The last message you sent and that I still have on my phone is "Good night, Momma, I love ya!"

Good night baby, I love you too.

Greg, his father, read:

Hey Maxie,

It's Dadio! But you already know that. I have so much I want to say to you. I'm not even sure where to begin. I think I'll just start with "I love you!" But I know you already know that too, don't you?

We said that a lot to each other when we were together. And we meant it, too. You'd say, "Love ya, Dadio" or "Love ya, Pops." Then we'd hug a big, old bear hug or high-five. I'd tell you to be safe or be careful and you'd just turn and look at me with that big smile. There was rarely a time we parted that we didn't say "Love you." It's just the way it was.I'm going to miss the things we did together, you, me, and your brother Ryan. We'd play cards, get the chips, play a little poker, Texas Hold 'em. It didn't really matter who won. Just to be together was enough. But, you did usually win. Don't know how you did that. We'd go fishing together. Well, we'd fish, Ryan would catch. Let's face it, Maxie, Ryan always was the fisherman in the family. But remember the last time we went fishing in Kentucky? You were the champion that day. I don't even think you needed any bait to catch a fish that day. The fish just seemed to jump into your arms.

That was fun. We would go golfing together. Man, you could really whack that little ball! It didn't always go straight, but it went! Remember that time on the golf course we huddled together in a porta-potty to take shelter from lightning and hail storm? Good call on that one, Maxie. We smelled like disinfectant for two days!

I loved the way you always stood up for the little guy or were willing to help someone in need. You hated bullies. And it didn't matter how big they were, either. They knew they had their hands full with Max Donahue. When you were growing up all the little kids like to "hang with you" because they felt they were safe. They knew you wouldn't let anything or anyone hurt them. You were their hero!

Most of all, I'm just going to miss you, your laugh, your passion and compassion and your love for life. You literally lived it to the "max." Up early, ready to take on the day, all day long. I love you, Maxie. We all love you. And we're all so very proud of you. And every American that values their freedom should be proud of you too for the way you so bravely served your country. I know at times, as a father I've let you down, but as a son you have never failed me. You're my hero!

God bless you, Maxie.

Love always, Dad

Letters from his high school teachers were also read.

Mr. Daley wrote:

One day, I am giving Max and Ryan a ride from school to Lone Tree in my 1995 Ford Escort station wagon, with one windshield wiper and half the controls on the dash missing. When we get on I-25 and hit about 55 mph, the car starts to shake because I have a busted rear spring. I turn to the boys to apologize, saying, "I really need to get this fixed."

Max looks at me, laughing, and says, "That's all right, Daley we know all about P.O.S's, (Piece of __its)!"

- *Max was a mighty warrior.*
- *Max was a mighty fisherman.*
- *Max was a fisher of men.*
- *Max was one fine young man.*

Max's good friend, Corporal Karim Rafghi, also spoke.

Rafghi's letter read:

Good afternoon. My name is Corporal Karim Rafghi. It is an honor to be asked to say a few words on behalf of Corporal Max William Donahue. He was and still is a friend, a brother and a fellow Marine. The first time I met Max was in a fight in K-9 School. There were so many of them and so few of us. I will never forget the picture of him standing there, surrounded by five guys. He was yelling and screaming at them, daring them to take a go at him. He was a fighter, and crazy at that. But that's what made him a good Marine and NCO [Non-commissioned officer].

Since I have known him, I have never known him to back down from anything. Max's first duty station was Hawaii and I was lucky enough to be stationed there with him. I could not imagine that place without him. He was one of the "go to" guys. If you wanted something done he got it done. He looked forward to training dogs in the Marines every day. I got into some trouble while I was in Hawaii. Max helped me to get back on the right path. The sad part is that I don't think I ever thanked him.

Max and I neared the end of our tour in Hawaii so we went onto Camp Pendleton to do one more deployment before we got out. He got that chance. I stayed back. Max, you were and always will be my best friend. Most people say this but I mean it. I would change places with you if I could, right now. What you taught, displayed and accomplished will not go unforgotten. You are loved by many and missed by all.

My dear friend Barb Whitfield sang the song "***If You Could See Me Now.***" It is one of the songs I had chosen to be sung at my funeral. How awful it was to be hearing it first at Max's. Barb sang with such emotion; it was as if she were singing a sermon.

One of the lines in the song is, "*If you could see me know, I'm standing tall and whole.*" I thought of Max standing, both legs and arm in-tact, and loved the sentiment that Max was doing great where he was and that we shouldn't worry. I believe to my core that heaven is a better place and that he is worry-free; that his beautiful body is whole again. I just miss him so.

As the funeral continued, I started feeling numb. I remember imagining myself speaking to Max, "What do you think, honey? I'm so sorry we have to do this."

A video montage of Max's life was played that included scenes from a DVD we received from Max the day after finding out he'd been killed. It was only the second mailing we had received from him in the two months he had been gone.

There was a scene where he and Fenji (his Marine dog) were going through a field in Afghanistan; his fellow Marines were in a straight line ahead of them. It also showed him filming a circle of his buddies getting high fives from one of the German Shepherds.

The last hand you see is Max's, as he lifts his hand to receive his high five from the dog. Time and time again, I've studied that picture, looking at my son's hand for the last time. And the final picture was of him standing in full gear, holding a big gun, with the words SEE YOU SOON -- I MISS YOU GUYS written in bold across the picture. And that was it. Fade back to the funeral. Fade back to the Marines escorting his coffin out of the chapel to the sound of *Amazing Grace*.

Garrett and Chad escorted me out of the chapel, followed by Ryan and Devan, family and friends. We were directed immediately into the limousines. We watched people exiting the chapel and pointed out those present to each other. As the limousines started to pull away, I heard the roar of the Patriot Guard's motorcycles and saw the flags waving from each bike. Until that moment, I had no idea that there were so many people present.

The funeral procession took back roads, as avoiding the highway is strongly recommended. At one point, we were trying to see the end of the procession and were not able to do so. I looked at Ryan and said, "You do know what he would be saying to you right now, don't you? How many cars are going to be in YOUR funeral procession, Ryan?" We knew he had us both beat.

The family plans the chapel service; the Marines plan the grave-site. And what a service it was. The Purple Heart presentation, the 21-gun salute, the folding and presenting of the flag -- it was all so surreal. I was watching, feeling numb, just participating in this event that was centered around my family. Everyone was there. In a way, I suppose that Max was there too.

We returned to the church afterward, for a reception. Then family and close friends were finally able to go back to the house. It was Friday, August 13, 2010, and I had just buried my son. What was to become of my life? Of Ryan's life? In my mind, it all started now. What "it all" meant, I didn't have a clue. But "it" was beginning.

Note -- part of the video can be seen on Max's website, maxdonahue.agi32.com, scroll to "more links," then "video."

And Max made three -- the odds were in our favor.

Although I'll never know for sure, I think Max got much of his confidence that he would not get hurt from sheer numbers. I've been told that only two other working dog handlers had died under hostile circumstances since 2002.

Sergeant Adam L. Cann was killed in action on January 5, 2006. He died in a suicide vest bombing at the Ramadi Glass Factory. Corporal Dustin Lee was killed in action on March 21, 2007. He died in a mortar attack on Camp Karma, Iraq. Max was the third working dog handler to be killed. The odds were so in our favor that he would return home to us. So many others had.

Also, Max was only the third military man to die from Highlands Ranch since Operation Iraqi Freedom. The boys and I lived in Highlands Ranch for many years prior to my second marriage. It's where they spent the majority of their school years. Max's name was the third to be added to the Highlands Ranch Veterans' Memorial.

When I consider the odds of what happened to Max, it makes me feel cheated. Although I would not wish this on anyone, why was it my Max who didn't come back? Sometimes I believe that the numbers lend credence to this being Max's destiny. It seemed we had so much in our favor in terms of his returning safely. But it was simply not to be. It is this subject that I can't dwell on too often. The unfairness to me, to Ryan, to Max, that this happened to us bewilders me. This is when I search for the "why?"

I do not believe that God was responsible for Max's dying, especially the horrible way that it happened. Scripture says that Satan is sitting on the throne of this world. 1 John 5:19, John 12:31, Luke 4:6, Ephesians 2:2, and John 16:11 all suggest this. I DO believe that God loved/loves Max as much and more than I do and that He loves me the same, as a parent loves a child.

I derive comfort from knowing the God in whom I fervently believe feels every inch of my pain and His heart aches as well. So many cannot understand the effect losing a child has on your life, nor do I want them to. But knowing that God understands better than anyone the pain of losing a son, provides great comfort. It makes me feel that I'm loved and not alone.

Ecclesiastes 9:4 states, "Anyone who is among the living has hope." So, until my time is up, hope it is!

Camp Pendleton, Camp Leatherneck and Camp Donahue

A little over a month after he died, Chad, Ryan, Greg and I attended a memorial for Max at Camp Pendleton. We met and spent time with the guys and gal who knew him, who had served with him. We visited the dog kennels and I saw Fenji, his dog in Afghanistan, for the first time. Even though I knew that the dog was not at fault, I carried resentment knowing that she had made it back yet my dear son had not. However, my emotions were mixed because I knew it would have pleased Max to know she had survived.

Note -- It was initially believed that Fenji had sight and hearing impairments. She was returned to Camp Pendleton and it was thought she would be retired. Fenji made a miraculous recovery and has since been returned to service.

To say that the memorial at Camp Pendleton was meaningful would not do justice to the experience. It was one more testament to the "Marines doing things right."

Letters were read from the unit with which Max was serving in Afghanistan.

A letter from one of his buddies read:

Max was instantly accepted into the unit, as if he was the missing piece. To say that Max had a magnetic personality would simply be an understatement. He came late into our lives and left in a hurry, but that's all it took and it made all the difference.

Before catching our flight to Denver, Gunny Smit and Corporal Webb were assigned to stay with Ryan and me. I'll never forget the sight of Corporal Webb coming into the lobby to meet us. He was dressed in a yellow vested suit against his dark skin, topped off with alligator skin shoes. Webb had served as a "sweep" with Max in Iraq, so he knew him well. He looked so handsome and dapper. I don't know if it was his intent, but I was flattered that he dressed up as he did. I had to assume that it was a sight not often seen on a Marine base.

Those last few hours, Gunny Smit and Corporal Webb drove Ryan and me around San Diego. Because the memorial service had been so emotional, I wanted to give Ryan a "happy thought" of our time there, so I arranged to rent a twenty-minute helicopter ride for the two of us.

The pilot had been a Marine twelve years earlier, and was generous with his time. He flew us over the San Diego Zoo and a nude beach (thank heaven the weather wasn't conducive to sun bathing) and we saw a whale underwater and closer in proximity to the beach than I thought was safe. Our pilot said that he had never seen a whale in the twelve years he had been flying. Was it an omen? I was grabbing at straws, anything to get a glimmer of hope or a "sign" from Max.

We then went to the San Diego pier. Gunny Smit and I walked together and were sharing our thoughts on what we'd experienced the past twenty-four hours. It was Gunny Smit who said to me, "It seems it's the good ones that go -- the best of the best that are taken." He went so far as to question his abilities, "If it's the best of the best, why am I still here?"

I had questions I wanted to ask about circumstances surrounding the attack in Afghanistan. Up to this point, the only official information I had received was on the Report of Casualty.

Under "Circumstances" the report read:

Hostile Action: Result of wounds received as a member of a dismounted patrol that was struck by an IED while conducting combat operations in the Helmand Province.

It went on to read:

Type:	Hostile
Status:	Deceased
Category:	Died of Wounds
Body Recovered:	Yes

There were still so many questions that had no answers. How did Max get off the field? Did someone have to carry him? Was there someone who saw what happened? Was anyone else hurt?

Gunny told me that Max was taken off the field on a gurney; no one had to carry him. There was someone with him who saw what happened. I know his name and hope to speak with him one day, only if and when he is ready and wants to. One other person was hurt but not killed.

When they brought us to the airport and we said our goodbyes, I felt heaviness in my heart and my stomach. I recalled the words read the day before at the memorial. One letter read that Max was like the missing piece of the unit's puzzle. "When he arrived it seemed as though everything fit."

I felt as though I would never be whole again. My life would never again fit as it should and I was leaving a piece of my life's puzzle in San Diego. A very big piece.

Another memorial was held at Camp Leatherneck in Afghanistan. We were sent a DVD of the service. I felt intense sadness listening to the readings and reflections of Max, not only for the words being spoken, but also for the sorrow in the voices speaking. These were the men and women who were truly putting their lives on the line every day, and the burying of one of their brothers was hitting awfully close to home. You could hear in their voices, there but for the grace of God go I.

One of the speakers, Max's Platoon Commander, 1st Lieutenant Shaun Locklear, read:

Very rare are leaders given the privilege to have a Marine under their charge like Corporal Max Donahue. Being Corporal Donahue's Platoon Commander, I was given that privilege. I can honestly say that he is the epitome of a Marine Non-Commissioned Officer.

I can still recall sitting in my office one day when I received a phone call. The voice on the other end identified himself as the Kennel Master stationed in Hawaii, and plainly stated, "Sir, I just wanted to give you a heads up on (2) Marines that have orders to your kennel at 1 MEF." I immediately thought the worse and braced myself for the unexpected.

He then stated that I will be receiving two of his best Marines and their names are Corporal Donahue and Corporal Rafghi and that these Marines were top-notch. He also stated that if he had 10 Donahues and 10 Rafghis, he could take over all of Afghanistan. Having the pleasure to serve with these Marines, I can vouch for those statements, especially Corporal Max Donahue.

I think dependability is a leadership trait that is often overlooked. It is hard to find those Marines who are dependable, time and time again. Each and every task that Max was given, he constantly stepped up to the plate and succeeded beyond my expectations. He was one of those exceptionally gifted Marines who had the ability to foresee an issue before it became a problem and correct the issue without any guidance or direction.

Having been in the Marine Corps for over 13 years, I think of myself as someone who is a pretty good judge of character. If there was a scale of best to worst, Corporal Donahue would be hands down at the top of the list. His unnerving ability to succeed at anything and everything made my life and job as the Platoon Commander much easier, sometimes too easy. We all know that a bored "LT" is never a good thing!

Since checking into the kennel, I have preached over and over to these Marines about family -- our K9 family. K9 is one of those unique brotherhoods that will open its arms to everyone. With numerous K9 Marines sitting in the audience today reflecting on their time and previous relationships with Max, it is truly a testament that our K9 family is honored to have served with Corporal Donahue and we are mourning the loss of one of our brothers.

Corporal Donahue, as I continuously look over some of the pictures taken back in Pendleton and also while here in Afghanistan, the only comfort I have is knowing that you gave your life doing something you loved to do -- being a K9 handler. No one will ever be able to put an exact number on either the lives you saved or the lives you touched; we can only assume it is an infinite number. Your ability to accomplish any mission at hand while constantly portraying that calm demeanor will never be forgotten. Myself and all your K9 brothers lost a piece of our heart on August 7th, but we smile knowing that you are currently patrolling the streets of heaven. I guarantee you will never be *lost, you will never be forgotten. We will honor your name and will always leave a seat for you at our K9 table.*

Semper FI

And then, the most touching of honors. There is a Camp Donahue in Afghanistan named after Max. Even without an extensive military background, I know that is a huge honor. I can only speculate, but I think the naming of Camp Donahue would have pleased Max greatly.

Tattoos

For me, getting a tattoo has never been a form of self expression. For my children, however, it is a favorite form; apparently for their friends as well. I think it is a sweet sentiment that, in almost every tattoo Max and Ryan got, they put the other's initials somewhere in it.

In a weak moment, I told Max that I would get a very small tattoo when he got back from Afghanistan. His failure to return was not the deal breaker for my not getting a tattoo.

During one of my morning Bible/prayer times I was thrilled to come across Leviticus 19:28, "Do not cut your bodies for the dead or put tattoo marks on yourselves." Neither one of my sons would expect me to go against a command in the Bible, even if it meant I would be breaking a promise.

I might have dodged the "tattoo bullet," but Max's brother, cousins, and friends went for it with gusto. The pictures that follow show some of the tattoos done in honor of Max.

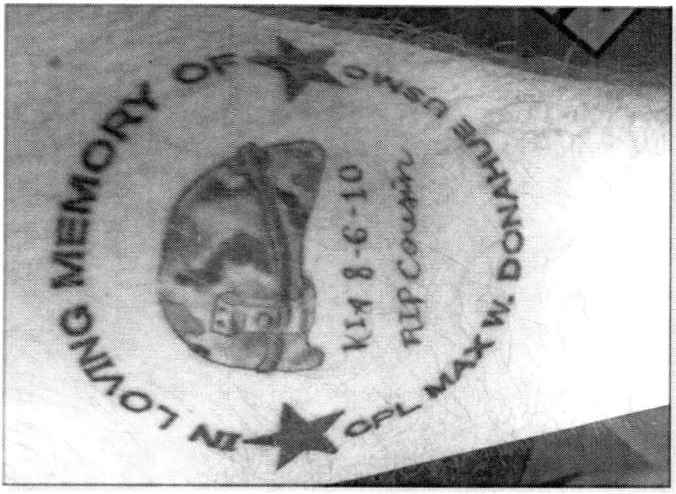

Cousin Dave and Ed's tattoo

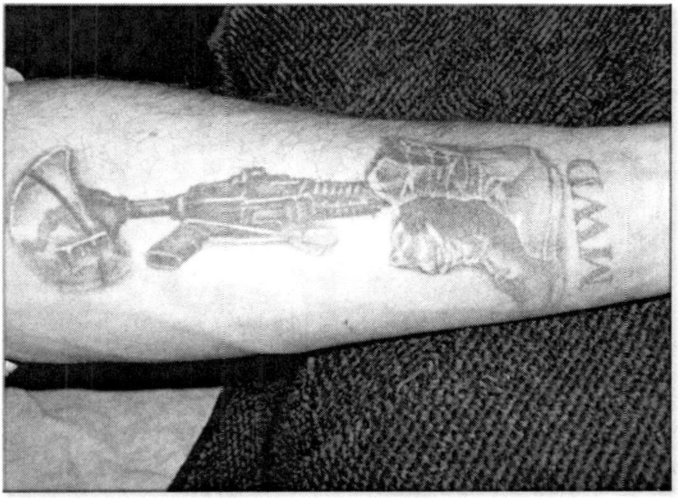

His brother Ryan's tattoo

His cousin Samantha expressed her feelings by adding to the butterfly tattoo already on her back:

Max's cousin Samantha's tattoo

Max's cousin Kim, being like-minded with me in opposition to getting a tattoo, found another form of expression. She found the hero bracelets and wears hers in place of a tattoo. I ordered 25! The bracelet reads:

In Loving Memory of CPL Max W Donahue
USMC 08/07/2010

My personal favorite from one of his Marine buddies, Barrywayne Walton:

Max's Marine friend Barrywayne Walton's tattoo. It's a reproduction of a picture of Max and his dog Paco, in Iraq.

My maternal favorite is easily the MWD, Max's initials' that Ryan put on his neck years before Max died. When we were at Max's memorial service at Camp Pendleton, I was walking with Gunny Smit and telling him that, the night before, Ryan started talking about joining the Marines. Of course, I panicked! Gunny quickly told me the tattoos on Ryan's neck would keep him out of the Marines because they were visible. Max, in this case his initials, were still protecting us.

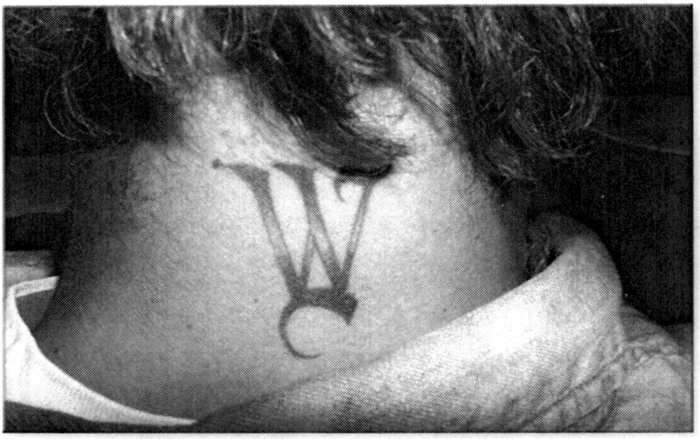

Ryan had Max's initials, MWD, tattooed on his neck. The M and D are under his ears.

Losing Garrett

Our CACO, Staff Sergeant Garrett Dorman, had been with us since the beginning. Garrett was responsible for the paperwork, communications, funeral, delivery of Max's body and the delivery of his personal belongings. Everything having to do with Max, his funeral and after the funeral, was Garrett's responsibility. What a job!

I became very attached to this man who took care of me when so much care was needed. I believe that he became attached to us as well. While at a Marine event in the mountains, he bought me a silver heart-shaped necklace with the Marine emblem in the middle and the words "Marine Mom" inscribed on the heart. It has become a cherished piece of jewelry.

I can't remember when I first learned that Garrett was going to retire from the Marines on November 1, 2010, after eight years of service. I do remember feeling as if I had been punched in the stomach. It felt like I was losing him too.

My final good-bye to Garrett was painful. Once again, I felt that horrible hole in my stomach. I was glad for him but also a little envious of the fact that he made it through his Marine experience while Max had not. He was going on to a new life and Max wasn't. He was going to college, and he had a wife and family; all the things I wanted for Max but would never get to see happen. Yes, I think it's fair to say I was jealous.

Garrett and I have kept in touch and I hope that we will always do so. The calls and e-mails will be farther and farther between, but I sincerely hope we don't lose track of each other.

Max's personal belongings

Three storage trunks, a collapsible desk and a television; that was the extent of my son's "personal effects." He had no car, no furniture, not a lot of possessions at all. Why should he until his life as a Marine was finished?

Garrett offered to stay with me and go through the trunks but I wanted to do it alone. This was my time with Max, another way of saying good-bye. It was another road I had to walk on the way to going on without him.

I'll never forget unwrapping a pair of his combat boots. His feet used to wear them; the feet that were attached to his legs that were amputated. I put the boots back in the trunk and left the room. That was enough for one day.

Later, as I continued through his things, I found his wallet. With shaking hands, I began to go through it. His wallet contained a worn letter from Jen, his girlfriend of six years. They were on the off-again side of their on-again, off-again relationship but off-again only because of timing. They were just too young. Max wanted to experience single life after the Marines. But, one thing I know for certain is that he loved Jen very much. Ryan knew it too.

I remember telling Jen that I thought theirs was the kind of love that could bring them back together in later years. Once they'd gotten older and experienced more of life, I thought it was very possible that they could find each other again. I felt love for this young woman who gave my son so much comfort. I could tell the letter had been read many times, and it meant a great deal to me, knowing it meant so much to Max. I put the letter in the "Jen" pile.

Max's main possessions were his X-box games and controls, and *Seinfeld, Family Guy* and *South Park* DVDs. The only others were his computer, camera and flat screen television. I found a journal in which he had written daily activities but it was difficult to understand. It was cryptic and written in Marine lingo.

When I showed it to Rafghi, he deciphered some of it for me. Apparently, daily activities need to be logged and, because there was no computer, he hand-wrote his notes. The writings began June 11, 2010, and entries were made every day up to July 4, 2010. I don't know why the writing stops so abruptly. Maybe he had access to a computer at that point. I was looking for personal notations but they weren't there to be found. I was still looking for a last word from Max.

Carefully, I continued through each wrapped object in the trunks; nothing could be thrown away, not yet anyway. It's all I have of him; a trunk full of "cammies," undershirts, socks, underwear; all military green or camouflaged. There were his civilian clothes, an envelope I addressed to him but with no letter inside, more dog tags, and then, the pictures I'd sent him from home. I scream. I cry. Is there nothing I can do to make this all stop?

Any little piece of information about Max was crucial. What was going on, what was he thinking? I was hungry for anything that could keep him alive and with me for just a little while longer. But it wasn't to be found. I found nothing that said he loved me. Nothing that said he was glad I was his mother. I knew it to be true, but wanted something in writing because I would never be able to hear it from him again.

It wasn't to be found, not in these belongings. But, then I remembered the letter he wrote to me on my 50th birthday. He was in some type of Marine training and was unable to be home for my party. His letter read:

Happy Birthday Mams.

What's on the other side of that massive hill (referring to my being over the hill)? I'm in my prime, so I wouldn't know.

You have no idea how much I miss you. I took your love for granted and I know now how much you deserve. But now things between us are perfect and I'll never look back. I'll always be there for you just like you're there for me.

I really dug myself into a "Man's World" (meaning the Marines) and it's hard to stay positive, but thinking of you makes things easy. It seems like I'm missing out on good memories we could be having, but I'll make up for them, I promise. I am so sorry I'm not there for your B-day but I am thinking about you, all day every day. You are the best mommy.

I love and miss all of you. See how many breaths you have to take to count from 1 to 50 (another crack on my age). I lost count.

--- lov ya ---

After reading it again I realized, I'd found it. It had been with me the whole time.

The autopsy

We received the autopsy report about three months after Max died. I didn't really read it at first; just sort of peeked at it and read only as much as I thought I could handle.

On the front of the envelope is the warning:

*It is **STRONGLY RECOMMENDED** that you read this in the presence of people that can provide you with emotional support during this time, such as your minister, a family friend or a counselor.*

My eyes landed on this sentence:

CPL Donahue was transported to Landstuhl Regional Medical Center in Germany with a diagnosis of catastrophic brain injury status post an improvised explosive device detonation.

I finally got my answer to the question asked so many times when all this first started, "How is his brain?" I don't recall being told about a brain injury, let alone a catastrophic one. Now I believe I wasn't meant to know, not then anyway.

Then I saw: Cause of Death: *Blast Injuries*

Manner of Death: *Homicide*

I also read:

The body is that of a well-developed male. The body weighs 132 pounds.

One hundred thirty-two pounds? I was certain that couldn't be right -- not with his muscles (guns, as he called his biceps) -- then I realized he was missing his legs and his right arm. I stopped reading and put the report away. It was simply more than I could handle. Again, will this ever stop?

Max's Organs Donated

One of the last pieces of correspondence we received from the Marines pertained to the donation of his organs. The letter read:

First of all, we wish to express our heartfelt condolences for the loss of your beloved son.

On August 6, 2010, Max died at the intensive care unit at Landstuhl Regional Medical Center in Germany in cause [sic] of his traumatic brain injury. According to his expressed will and the will of the family, you gave consent to organ donation. You agreed to harvest those organs being appropriate for transplantation purposes. Now we wish to inform you about the course of events.

After intensive investigation of the medical preconditions, the liver and both kidneys were, as regulated by German law, reported to the Foundation EUROTRANSPLANT in Leiden/Netherlands. On EUROTRANSPLANTS' waiting list are potential organ recipients from Germany and six other European countries. EUROTRANSPLANT is responsible for the mediation and allocation of organ donation procedures and procures the organs to the transplantation centers regarding urgency of transplantation, chance of success and time on waiting list.

Max's liver helped a 34-year-old man. This patient had been on EUROTRANSPLANT waiting list since December 2009. He was suffering from cirrhosis with liver failure. Now the function of the transplanted liver is good and the patient is getting well again. You saved his life by giving consent to organ donation.

The right kidney was transplanted to a 67-year-old man who had a renal failure based on chronic glomerulonephritis. The man waited for transplantation for over ten years. Dialysis is not necessary anymore because the renal function of the transplanted kidney is good.

The left kidney was transplanted to a 14-year old boy in Croatia. Renal failure made dialysis necessary up to the time the transplantation was done. Renal failure was caused by inflammation. The function of the transplanted kidney and the medical condition of the patient are brilliant.

I've been asked if I would like to meet the recipient's of Max's organs. I don't. I am glad that something positive came from Max's death. I'm glad for the recipients and their families. But it won't bring him back to me. I don't want to be in the presence of Max's kidneys; I want to be with Max.

Although there is nothing I want more than having Max back, short of that, there are still things I want. One is for people to seriously consider their faith and accept Christ into their life. If lives are saved, either by organ donation or eternally by confessing Christ as their Savior, there would be meaning to losing Max. It would be an answer to the question, "Why?"

Getting through the "firsts"

21st Birthdays

Why did the first birthday without Max have to be Taylor's 21st, just 4 days after Max died? Then Devon, his cousin (Judy's daughter), turned 21 the following week. And Ryan's 21st was on November 1st.

I am certain that when the boys talked about how they would celebrate Ryan and Taylor's 21st birthdays, there was a lot of drinking and partying planned. The actual celebrations were much more mellow.

For Ryan's birthday we met at *The Stagecoach*, a bar across from where he worked. It was a Monday night and seemingly low key. I was glad it wasn't crowded and I noticed that the pool tables were open. Several friends joined us and we ate pizza and played pool. Ryan drank beer, legally. He was home at 8:45 and because he had to be at work at 6:00 am, went to bed shortly thereafter. Again, not exactly the stuff most 21st birthdays are made of.

No one spoke it, but it was obvious that we were thinking about Max and what he and Ryan had always meant to each other. What a different night this would have been for Ryan, if Max had been alive. I thought about how Ryan would never get to live out so many of the experiences he would have shared with his brother. I felt so very bad for him. Everything seems different now. Because everything IS different now. We all have to get used to feeling what it's like to live without Max.

There is some comfort in knowing Max would not have been here physically for the birthdays anyway. He was in Afghanistan -- or would have been. How he would have made his presence known, and he undoubtedly would have, we will never know.

November 10, 2010 – Happy 235th Birthday, Marine Corps

Let me assure you that, before this year, I did not know that November 10 was the birth date of the Marine Corps. However, I think that it is important to mention how I made this discovery.

Judy and I were in Ft. Lauderdale, Florida, visiting her mother. Judy was staying on a few days longer and it was the day I was to leave. We stopped at a sidewalk café prior to going to the airport. It seemed unusual to me that the bartender, a gentleman who looked to be in his mid-fifties, was wearing a Marine T-shirt. Then I noticed that the two gentlemen at the bar were wearing

Marine hats and had Marine wallets. And the hostess was wearing a military shirt. Everywhere I looked, tragically, Marine, Marine, Marine!

This seemed like a cruel, not-so-funny joke. Judy even noticed it because, when I came back from using the restroom, she had switched places with me in hopes I wouldn't be seeing "everything Marine." I said to her, "You see it too!"

It wasn't until I got in the car and headed to the airport that I received an e-mail from one of Max's buddies wishing Max, through me, a Happy 235th Marine Birthday. I was relieved to think there was an explanation, separate from my loss, for the "everything Marine in my face."

Christmas

The first Christmas without Max came and went. Christmas has always been a big deal in my house. I put lights on anything near an electrical outlet, inside and outside. This year, I decorated, bought presents and tried to maintain some sense of normalcy.

For the last few years, I would bring out the decorations and think we were one year closer to when Max would be out of the Marines and able to spend Christmas with us. You can easily imagine what I thought this year.

The things that I could not bring myself to do were two of my favorites, baking cookies and listening to my Christmas music. I have six Christmas CDs that I listen to over and over; the boys and Chad would get annoyed because I would play them so often. I didn't even listen to them once. And I still haven't baked a cookie. I know I'll do these things again, but not now, not this first year.

I chatted with a neighbor who had lost her husband the year before. She said she hated the Christmas season and just wanted it to be over. I remember thinking that Christmas was the time we celebrated the birth of Jesus who, without his birth and death, we wouldn't have the promise of eternal life in heaven. How could I not celebrate the birth of the person whose life made it possible for me to be with Max again? It was, and is, the only hope that I have. Having no joy around the Christmas season was something that I was not going to let the devil take away from me. He had taken enough.

My neighbor gave me a poem that I have vowed to read every Christmas at Max's grave. Although several sources are cited, the writing of the poem is attributed to a 13-year-old boy named Ben, who died of a brain tumor in 1997. He gave the poem to his mother prior to his death.

My First Christmas in Heaven

I see the countless Christmas trees around the world below,
With tiny lights, like heaven's stars, reflecting on the snow.
The sight is so spectacular; please wipe away that tear;
For I am spending Christmas with Jesus Christ this year.
I hear many Christmas songs that people hold so dear;
But the sounds of music can't compare with the Christmas voice up here.
I have no words to tell you the joy their voices bring,
For it is beyond description to hear the angels sing.
I know how much you miss me. I see the pain inside your heart,
But I am not so far away. We really aren't apart.
So be happy for me, dear ones. You know I hold you dear;
And be glad I'm spending Christmas with Jesus Christ this year
I send you each a special gift from my heavenly home above.
I send you each a memory of my undying love.
After all, love is the gift, more precious than pure gold.
It was always most important in the stories Jesus told.
Please love and keep each other as my Father said to do.
For I can't count the blessing or love He has for each of you.

So have a Merry Christmas and wipe away that tear;
Remember, I'm spending Christmas with Jesus Christ this year.

Up to the point of reading that poem, I had only considered MY first Christmas without Max. I then realized that it was his first one away from us and, after reading the poem, felt a little more at peace on this earth.

Max's Unit Returns -- December 26, 2010 – My "Difference" Date

Things were getting harder for me as we approached the day his unit would return from Afghanistan. They got back on December 26, 2010, the date my life really started to be different. Up to that point, my-day-to-day had not changed very much, except for the phone calls and letters I would have received from Max, but didn't. But now, he would have been home.

Afghanistan was to have been Max's last deployment. After his return, he would have only had seven months remaining in the Marine Corp. He would then be ours again.

As of December 26, I had to start dealing with the lack of Max's presence in my life; his physical presence that would have been at the kitchen table or in the car with us. He would never be here for me or Ryan, Taylor, Jen, Devan, for so many, as we had all hoped. I would never see him get married, or have children, or grow old.

I had planned on being at Camp Pendleton when he got off the plane to celebrate his last deployment. Now, my heart hurts with the pain of so many things I won't be doing or experiencing. For me, the real pain of Max being gone began again on December 26, and will be with me every day that follows.

Note -- I have since found out that the possibility of his re-enlisting was greater than he led me to believe. Wise move as, if I was Max, I would not have wanted to tell me he was re-enlisting either.

New Year 2011

As I have said, many things changed for me after December 26; the sadness seemed to be getting deeper. Only five months had passed, and it felt that the way I was dealing with Max's death was beginning to go in the wrong direction. I knew that I would not let my sadness get too extreme, but had to monitor the depth that I was willing to let it go.

I prayed about what Max's legacy would be -- the one I hoped for -- that through his death, people would give their lives to the Lord. That would be my greatest comfort and a way that I could make sense of his dying, so young and so strong, so dear and so sweet.

I will strive to live for others in the name of Max and, more importantly, in the name of Jesus. Sorry Satan, but Max's death has brought me even closer to God. And my loss will prayerfully bring others into the kingdom as well. I get fired up, thinking that Satan picked the wrong family to mess with. I know he picked the wrong mother!

Tomorrow

I don't know how many tomorrows there will be for me. I have to admit, I care less than I did before August 7. No plans to get to heaven sooner than God intends, it's just that heaven is where I'll get to see Max and Jesus, and I look forward to being with both. Of course, that would mean leaving Ryan and Chad and that is NOT something to which I look forward. But Ryan and Chad both believe in Jesus, so whatever time we spend apart will be temporary. And, in all fairness to me, I had better be the next one to go. I don't ever want to be the funeral planner again.

Life now holds a new sense of urgency. I've seen and lived the difference between a funeral for someone who knew and confessed Jesus as their Savior and someone who did not. The entire atmosphere is different, and I believe that difference is hope. Hope and the belief, not just the wish, but the absolute knowing that we will be with our loved ones again.

Life is so different from what it was before. Being an insurance broker has lost some of its luster! I understand more than ever how precious life is. And by life, I mean the involvement that we have with our family, friends, neighbors and community.

There will be days when I'll choose to give in to the sadness, ideally, less and less as time goes on. I hope that on the sad days, I have the opportunity to stay home, be away from people and cry it out by myself.

Like it or not, life is moving on. My tomorrows will be very different from my yesterdays, but they will be what I want them to be, inasmuch as I can choose to experience joy or not. Either way, I make the choice.

What about your tomorrows? Whether or not you decide to go on a quest to consider accepting Jesus as your Savior, how are you choosing to live your life? What impact are you having on those around you? How are you making the world a better place to live? What do you want your legacy to be? The answering of these questions should not be postponed, as no one is assured that tomorrow will come.

By the way

I asked a friend who served as a Security Policeman in the Air Force for twenty-four years what he thought of the events surrounding Max's death, and he said, "Americans don't have a clue what freedom costs."

I know what he means; military families also know but for many Americans, they aren't touched by freedom not being free. Freedom comes at a huge price, to those who seek it, to those who value it and to those who protect it. Until recently, I didn't understand it either.

The price of freedom can take many forms – loss of time together, loss of limbs and loss of loved ones. "Freedom isn't free" is not merely a bumper sticker. It's a fact of life that many Americans, like my family and I have to live out. Freedom is not free and for me, freedom is not fair.

Help me understand how any American, how any person, can tolerate a group of people protesting at the funeral of a fallen soldier. Really? Why did we have to have the Patriot Guard at Max's funeral? Just in case? Was it in case some people thought their right to protest and to voice their cause was more important than my family's right to bury our loved one?

Don't speak to me about the right of free speech, especially when it overrides my right to bury my child in peace. Can we please all agree on this one?

And, because I'm on a roll, it certainly doesn't feel as though Americans appreciate the cost of their freedom when the pledge of allegiance no longer begins each school day, or standing for the flag is no longer standard practice. And what about the people who talk while the national anthem is being sung? What's that all about? There are young men and women dying in service to this country and you can't stop your conversation long enough to sing the national anthem? Or at least be quiet for it? Hmmm.

Military Courage

Recently, there was a news report about a 13-year old boy who had been chased and beaten up by a group of eleven other boys. The horror of it all was video-taped and, not only did you witness the atrocity taking place, but you also watched a woman crossing the street, totally ignoring his cries for help. It did not appear as though she even considered helping. And, no, it wasn't because she was unaware of what was taking place.

Anyone watching that newscast witnessed an innocent 13-year old boy being brutally beaten by a gang of thugs and although others knew what was happening, no one came to his aid.

It struck me that this is what our military fights for. Remember my Scottish "angel on the plane" who said that it's the American military that steps in to protect the world? I was watching this horrible scene where the one who was weak was being brutally overtaken while onlookers stood idly by. It brought to mind Saddam Hussein's Iraq and Hitler's Germany. Our military did not and does not stand idly by. Max would ABSOLUTELY have intervened. So would have Ryan. And I have to hope that anyone reading this book, and I, would have as well.

I believe that one of the gifts Max left behind is his example of courage to correct the wrongs going on around him; to step in and help someone in need. As an individual, Max was an example of courage; being a Marine gave him the outlet and the opportunities to display that courage. I just wish we had more time to witness it.

My Hope for Max's Legacy

What was Max's legacy? We don't know yet. I would be interested in hearing how he would want that question answered.

Right now, my answer is this: Max was very charismatic and, even as a young boy, seemed to draw people to him. He believed in Jesus Christ as his Lord and Savior and confessed so on several occasions. Ryan has reassured me of Max's belief.

As his mother, I would like to think that his charisma was put to good use; that the young people who knew Max would now realize that death can happen any day. Max died so young and strong and with so much for which to live. If death can happen to him, it could happen to anyone, at any time.

My hope is that Max's death launches twenty-somethings on a quest to find their own truth; seeking answers to questions such as, what happens after this life, who is Jesus and what do I believe?

Max's legacy will be determined by the people whose lives he touched and what they do with the impact of having known him. My hope is that people will consider Christ when otherwise, they may not have.

I also hope that, when people remember Max, they derive strength from his courage and a desire to help anyone who needs it; that they look for ways to lend a hand. I am so proud of who Max was and how he helped others. This world needs more Maxes.

Max, Ryan and I. This is a favorite picture of ours.

Our 2009 family Christmas picture, the last one we have with Max

My favorite picture of the brothers, taken on Max's last visit with us.

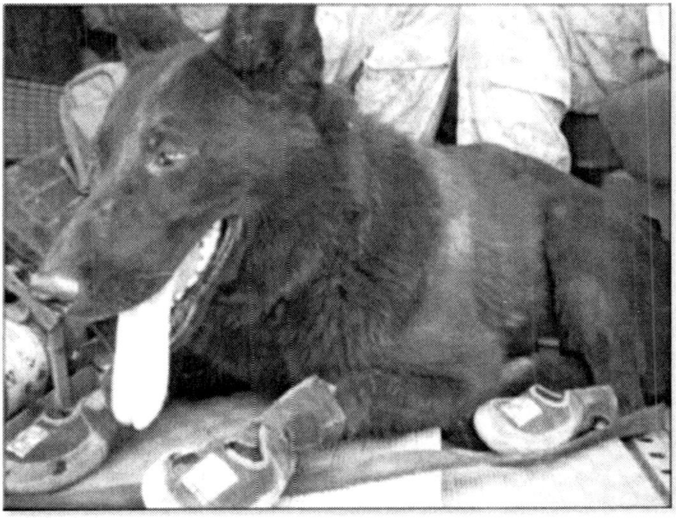

Max's dog in Afghanistan, Fenji.
Notice the booties to protect her paws from the heat.

Max in Afghanistan

The last picture on the DVD Max mailed us from Afghanistan. We received it the day after he died.

The front of Max's headstone

Back of Max's headstone

Picture of his Marine buddies mourning at Camp Leatherneck

Another shot from his memorial at Camp Leatherneck

The poster was drawn by Cpl Shoemaker and Cpl Brenner in Afghanistan. The wall stands 7 feet tall and the Memorial was completed with a pencil and then outlined with marker. It was placed at the entrance of the kennel compound at Camp Leatherneck, later at the entrance of Camp Donahue.

The entrance of Camp Donahue in Afghanistan

Raising the flag at Camp Donahue

Max's unit the day they left Afghanistan on their way back home

Section II

Finding hope and strength

How to live, really live, after the death of a loved one.

It's difficult for me to describe life during the months immediately following Max's death. My family experienced a whirlwind of activities and tributes to him; memorials, letters, messages and hand-made from-the-heart items from people around the country, expressing support and prayer. Their letters express heartache for the loss of their loved ones; stomach-wrenching, gut-punching pain that remains with them, years after their loss.

A friend of mine attended a support group for people who had lost their spouses. One woman, who was new to the group and had recently lost her husband, asked, "Does it ever get better, does the pain subside?" Three people in the group responded, "No."

When my friend told me this, I was shocked. Where was the "support" in that group? I thought to myself, "That is not going to be me; I won't let myself be miserable for the rest of my life."

I remembered when I was at my kitchen table, picking out Max's coffin and cremation urn, when Garrett passed the pictures to me and I withdrew. It was the moment when I pictured Max's face looking at me, and feeling him say, "Don't disappoint me,

Momma. Somebody has to do this and you're the one I picked. Don't make me sorry for that decision."

That was the time when I knew I would get through this; and I mean ALL of this. Not just the coffin-picking and funeral-planning, but my life, the whole rest of my life.

I think of it like this:

If your loved one had two minutes to talk to you, and you weren't allowed to say anything, what would they say? Would they be pleased with how you were living your life? Would they be proud of how you were remembering their life and their love for you?

During my two minutes with Max I would want to hear,

"Mom, I'm doing great up here. You won't believe how wonderful it is. Good job on the funeral. All is well with me. And Mom, thank you. Thank you for continuing to live and still be happy. Thank you for not letting this ruin your life. You didn't let me down and I'm proud of you. Watch out for Chad, Ryan and Taylor for me. See you soon."

It is a conscious decision to move my mind (actually my heart) to that place. The place where I choose to go on each and every day.

When I'm going through a weak moment, I literally visualize his face, talking to me and saying, "Mom, I'm doing great up here." I hear it over and over, "Thank you for not letting this ruin your life."

I've come to realize how strong the gift of choice is. How I enter into each day, how I live the moments, are really my choices. The attitude I choose will get me through, for the good or for the bad. It's my choice.

When my feet hit the ground each morning, I can choose to be sad or I can make it a point to find some joy in the day. No one and nothing, not even Max's death, can take that from me. Maybe it can be removed temporarily, but only temporarily. And only if I let it.

Please understand, I am not discounting or minimizing the pain that comes after the death of a loved one. Of course there is sorrow, deep sorrow. And there is no stopping its arrival. What I can do is determine how far I'll let it take me down. There are days I go down pretty far. But those days are getting fewer and farther between. And the depth of the sorrow is not as deep, or perhaps it's a different type of sorrow that evolves through time.

I believe that it is more difficult to be happy than to remain in sadness. Sadness doesn't take as much effort. Getting out of bed, out of the house, socializing with others, THAT all requires effort.

If I was the one who died would I want my death to ruin Max or Ryan's life, or Chad's or anyone whom I loved? Absolutely not. I would want them to remember me, to talk about me and to live their lives with even more purpose than before. And if they had not given their lives to God, if they hadn't confessed Jesus as their Lord and Savior, I would want them to start considering it.

Getting through grief -- Being "okay plus."

Several months after Max's death, my sister asked me how I was doing. I said, "I think I'm 'okay plus.'"

Being the daughter of a teacher, I like to put a grade on things. "Okay plus" meant I was doing a little better than average, given someone in my circumstance.

Although I'm still a work in progress, I feel that I'm doing okay and will continue in the upward direction.

I find that realization odd, as I had always thought that the death of either one of my sons would destroy me. It was always the unimaginable thought to think. Now, when people ask how I am, I answer, "Better than I ever thought I would be." And it's true.

It's written somewhere that, "Until we die, we are expected to live." After having lost one of the two most precious parts of my life, I vow to continue living and to have happiness in my life. It may not be as joyful as it once was, but there is still joy to experience.

When I thought about how any of that can be true, how it is that I'm not drowning in sorrow, I began writing down what the components are to my thinking I am "okay plus."

Before I expound on how I am handling my grief, it is extremely important for me to clarify one point. As I was in the process of writing this book, one of my prayers was, "Please don't let what I write be hurtful in any way."

I did not and don't want to portray an attitude of, "I'm getting through it, why aren't you?" Please understand, that is NOT what I am saying. My writings are in no way meant to be a criticism or judgment on how others handle their grief.

Grief is as personal as the feelings we experience for those who have left us. By that definition, neither anyone else nor I have the ability (or the right) to dictate the methods by which others grieve.

What I am attempting to communicate is this: there is much mourning, sorrow and grief that accompanies the death of a loved one. And, we all have different methods for dealing with the process. But as much as possible, attempt to live the life that your loved one would want for you. Don't let your sadness become the definition of who you are. Your loved one would not have wanted you to stop living because of his or her death.

The points that follow are, what I believe, the components that help me to be "okay-plus."

1. FAITH

My loved one had confessed Jesus as his Lord and Savior. I believe that Max was heaven-bound. I have a faith to carry me through and give me hope, hope that we will be together again.

2. HOPE

Along those same lines, I've given my life to the Lord and confessed him as my Savior. I know where I am going and whom I'll see when I get there. Hope never leaves me.

3. LOVE

Max knew that he was loved and we knew that he loved us. Every day and every phone call had "I love you" within it.

We were and are an affectionate bunch. The women in Max's life got hugs and his arm around their shoulders; the men were wrestled to the ground. And Ryan, whom I believe Max loved most, bore the brunt of that love. When Max and Ryan were together, there was always blood and bruising, but gratefully, never a broken bone. I remember frequently yelling, "If either of you get hurt, I'll take you to the doctor but you'll pay the doctor bill!"

"I love you;" we said it and showed it often.

4. MAX'S CHOICE

Max was doing what he wanted to do, what he chose to do. I tried to talk him out of going to Afghanistan, and so did others. Max was not only a Marine; he was also his own man. He would not be talked out of going.

When we were at Camp Pendleton for his memorial, Gunny Smit told me that he did not have to decide who was going on that mission to Afghanistan. He had to decide who was staying behind. All the Marines under his command wanted to be sent. I find that to be a testament to the strength and character of those men and women. And to my Max.

5. COMMUNICATION

We talked about what he wanted, "in case" -- burial versus cremation, whom he wanted to inherit what, etc. I had a good idea of what his choices were because we had talked about them. Before he left for Iraq, he told me that he was leaving everything in my name and I could make the decisions.

I remember saying, "Oh no, I don't think so. You tell me what you want and I'll do it -- maybe!" I said, "You are not pinning that one on me!"

And so, we had a brief talk about his choice to be cremated, what he wanted done with the life insurance money, personal effects, etc. I am very glad that we had that talk, difficult though it was. It helped me tremendously when I actually had to communicate and direct his decisions.

Note -- Max wanted to be cremated and his ashes spread over the Rocky Mountains of Colorado. I obliged him as far as the cremation but buried his ashes in the cemetery where I too, will be buried. Given the comfort it gives me to have a place to go and be with him, I don't think he would have minded.

6. HE'S WATCHING ME

I've said it before but it bears repeating. I picture him watching the way that I respond to situations and events and I want to make him as proud of me as I am of him.

It's the "two-minutes with him talking to me and I can't say anything" scenario. When I die, I want to hear, "Well done" from Jesus and from Max. I don't want to fail either one of them.

Knowing these things keep me "okay plus," and may eventually get me to "good."

May I suggest ... just in case

When a loved one is gone, they are gone forever. Any and all opportunities to right a wrong, say "I love you," forgive a transgression, all go with the loved one who has died. So, may I suggest you consider, "What do I need to say or do just in case I don't see my loved one again? What if they died tonight? What if I died tonight?"

Before suggesting anything, I'd like to clarify; I'm not a psychologist, a pastor, or a therapist. My degree is in Social Welfare from the Ohio State University and I've never used it professionally. I am simply a mother of two sons whom I love dearly. Now only Ryan can dispute my maternal competence.

When I look back on our lives as the boys were growing up, I think of times we shared and how those reflections are now of great comfort to me. Based on that, the following are thoughts and suggestions for you to consider, on what I am glad I did in the past that consoles me now as I experience the grieving process.

1. Write letters to your loved ones. When the boys were little, I wrote each of them a letter in the event that I died. I still have both in my safe deposit box. How sad it made me to see the letter I wrote to Max and realized that it would never be read as intended. However, had I gone first, Max would have had and Ryan does have, my last letter to each of them.

You hear it so often. People who have lost a loved one, just want one more moment, one more chance to tell them how much they are loved and what significance their lives had. With an "in case I die" letter, you have that one last "I love you."

My letters tell the boys what I think their God-given strengths are, how special I think they are and what they exhibit that makes me feel as I do. They tell them my hopes for what their lives will become and what kind of men I hope they grow to be. And they get to read one more time, how proud I am to be their mother and how much I love them. They have these words to own and to read whenever, forever.

2. Live a little bit more like you were dying. Don't go into debt but if you have money, spend some of it. Make memories, go on vacations, take road trips; do anything to spend time with those you love in ways that are different from the norm, away from all the unimportant, attention-diverting issues that take priority over giving time to those who are special to you.

Money is something I haven't had a lot of but I am very glad that we let loose of some of it and took the boys to Mexico before Max went into the Marines. Chad and I are still hearing stories of the boys' escapades that took place after he and I had said good-night. It was worth every penny, especially now.

3. And may I suggest, just in case, that you think about your faith. Take seriously the thought of your death, or a loved one's. Imagine that it could happen tomorrow. What do you believe? Where would you derive your comfort? What hope do you have?

If you are unsure of your answers, there are many good books on these topics. Lee Strobel's book, <u>The Case for Christ; A Journalist's Personal Investigation of the Evidence for Jesus,</u> is one. Lee's journey began as an atheist attempting to gather the information needed to convince his Christian wife into giving up her faith, or at least toning it down. He did extensive, factual research in his quest to derive his own answers to the aforementioned questions.

The ultimate source is the Bible. Start with the New Testament as it speaks to the hope and salvation Christ gives. And anything by Billy Graham is worth reading.

Many memories, few regrets

When I reflect on those few, precious years I had as a parent (that we all have as parents) I'm grateful to have few regrets What I do have are precious memories of times spent with the boys. Now, those memories are all that I have of Max.

Some of the times that I cherish, that I am so very glad we did, and that I would like to share, are:

1. Teach your children to date. When Max and Ryan turned thirteen, I had each of them take me out on a date. It was a pretend date where I showed them what I look for in someone who took me out. Hold the door, pull out my chair, treat the wait staff with respect, put your napkin in your lap and tip generously.

If the woman they were dating did not want that treatment, the way she communicated that to them would be evidence of her character. If she was kind and respectful, she had second date potential. If she was abrupt, cut her loose!

2. Play games. Throughout the years, we frequently played games. There are games that I associate with periods of time in our lives. There are the Sorry years, the Yahtze years, and the Catch Phrase and poker years.

It was a great way to see Max and Ryan's personalities develop and watch how they related to each other. Max wanted to win; Ryan wanted to make us laugh (and he did).

3. Play music. Have songs that, when heard, you think of your loved one and they think of you. Take ownership of songs that bring back memories of times together and fun that was shared.

There are songs that, when I hear them, I will always think of Max. When the boys were young, we would go on road trips, sometimes just to a hotel with a swimming pool where we would swim until night then bring out the board games.

Before each trip, we'd buy a CD to play in the car, over and over, until we knew all the words. We did that intentionally so that anytime we heard the songs later, we'd remember our trip.

You get the idea. Take the time to play and laugh together. Make memories you can reminisce about and cling to later.

What I know

One thing that I know is this; life comes with bumps and bruises, broken promises and broken hearts. But God is there to get us through the very toughest of times, if we let Him. God has carried me through every moment of this ordeal. That I know for sure.

Another thing that I know is that war is truly hell, on everyone involved. I have to believe that this is true for both sides. Rafghi told me that when Max's unit returned, the young Marine who witnessed Max being hit by the IED, went "ghost." I asked him what that meant. He said that as soon as they landed, he disappeared. He left immediately. I can't imagine what this young Marine saw or the vision that he sees when he thinks about the events of that day.

I hope to speak with that young Marine, if and when he is ready, only to let him know that Max's family is doing okay and that I hope he is as well. I want to know that what he saw has not overtaken his spirit.

I know there are many others with similar visions. I can't imagine being so close to death, let alone witnessing it. And these deaths are not quiet, nor are they gentle.

Listening to conversations between veterans in the waiting room of the Veteran's Administration, you hear that the sights of war can ruin lives. I don't want that for the Marine who witnessed Max getting hurt. And neither would Max.

One last thing that I know for sure is that I loved my son with all my heart. I love my sons with all my heart. Ryan and I, his father Greg, Chad, Taylor and Jordan, all those who loved him and who love us, will live the rest of our lives without Max. There will be no new stories to tell, only memories of the fun we had and what we did with him in our past. Is that enough? It has to be. It has to be because it's all that we've got. We have that and our hope and belief that we will all be together again.

Good night baby, I love you

The rest of my life will be spent missing Max. When the family gets together, there will always be a gnawing feeling that something isn't quite right, that Max isn't there with us. Even though I'll never enjoy another 100% day in this lifetime, those happiest of days spent with my husband and all of my children, I believe there are 95% days in my future.

I'll get my 100% back once I reach heaven.

As I said in my letter to Max that was read at the funeral;

I know we'll be together again, honey, I truly do.

It will be a long rest of my life without you, but I'll trade it for eternity with you.

Good night baby, I love you.

Section III

Inspiration

In the Words of Others

There were, and still are, so many things and people that are helping me get through this period of my life. I'd like to share phrases and sayings that have been sources of strength, hope and comfort throughout my ordeal.

Some people spend an entire lifetime wondering if they made a difference in the world. But, the Marines don't have that problem.

Ronald Reagan, President of the United States; 1985

Freedom is not free, but the U.S. Marine Corps will pay most of your share.

Ned Dolan

You cannot exaggerate about the Marines. They are convinced to the point of arrogance, that they are the most ferocious fighters on earth -- and the amusing thing about it is that they are.

Father Kevin Keaney
1st Marine Division Chaplain
Korean War

We few, we happy few, we band of brothers;
For he today that sheds his blood with me;
Shall be my brother.
Shakespeare, 'Henry V'

Everybody can be great... because anybody can serve. You don't have to have a college degree to serve. You don't have to make your subject and verb agree to serve. You only need a heart full of grace, a soul generated by love."
Martin Luther King, Jr.

Being a hero is about the shortest-lived profession on earth.
Will Rogers

Now the trumpet summons us again -- not as a call to bear arms, though arms we need; not as a call to battle, though embattled we are; but a call to bear the burden of a long twilight struggle, year in and year out, 'rejoicing in hope, patient in tribulation', a struggle against the common enemies of man: tyranny, poverty, disease and war itself.
John F. Kennedy

A man does what he must – in spite of personal consequences, in spite of obstacles and dangers and pressures – and that is the basis of all morality.
John F. Kennedy

There are only two lasting bequests we can hope to give our children. One of these is roots, the other, wings.
Hodding Carter

Of all animals, the boy is the most unmanageable!
Plato

The future is purchased by the present.
Samuel Johnson

Almighty God; Our sons, pride of our nation, this day have set upon a mighty endeavor, a struggle to preserve our Republic, our religion and our civilization, and to set free a suffering humanity.

Lead them straight and true; give strength to their arms, stoutness to their hearts, steadfastness in their faith … Their road will be long and hard. For the enemy is strong … Success may not come with rushing speed, but we shall return again and again; and we know by Thy grace, and by the righteousness of our cause, our sons will triumph …

With Thy blessing, we shall prevail over the unholy forces of our enemy. Help us to conquer the apostles of greed and racial arrogances. Lead us to the saving of our country, and with our sister nations into a world unity that will spell a sure peace – a peace invulnerable to the schemings of unworthy men. And a peace that will let all men live in freedom, reaping the just rewards of their honest toil.

From Franklin D. Roosevelt's D-Day Address, June 6, 1944

Hope in the Word

While going through the process of grieving, I did and do a lot of reading and have found great hope from various authors as I read their words of encouragement and hope. But, the greatest source of strength that I get is from reading my Bible and praying every day.

The following are passages from Scripture that help get me through my new life without Max.

Anyone who is among the living has hope.
Ecclesiastes 9:4

And God will wipe away every tear from their eyes.
Revelation 7:17

For God so loved the world that he gave his one and only Son, that whoever believes in him shall not perish but have eternal life.
John 3:16

Jesus said to her, "I am the resurrection and the life. He who believes in me will live, even though he dies, and whoever lives and believes in me will never die."
John 11:25

Greater love has no man than this, that he lay down his life for his friends.
John 15:13

Now faith is being sure of what we hope for and certain of what we do not see.
Hebrews 11:1

Brothers, we do not want you to be ignorant about those who fall asleep, or grieve like the rest of men, who have no hope. We believe that Jesus died and rose again and so we believe that God will bring with Jesus those who have fallen asleep in him.
1 Thessalonians 4:13, 14

I have fought a good fight, I have finished my course, I have kept the faith.
2 Timothy 4:7

Oh my father, if it possible, let this cup pass from me: nevertheless, not as I will, but as thou wilt.
Matthew 26:39

Weeping may remain for a night
But rejoicing comes in the morning
Psalm 30:5

"I tell you the truth", Jesus said to them, "no one who has left home or wife or brothers or parents or children for the sake of the kingdom of God will fail to receive many times as much in this age and, in the age to come, eternal life."
Luke 18:29, 30

I consider that our present sufferings are not worth comparing with the glory that will be revealed in us.
Romans 8:18

Do not let your hearts be troubled. Trust in God, trust also in me. In my Father's house are many rooms; if it were not so, I would have told you. I am going there to prepare a place for you. And if I go and prepare a place for you, I will come back and take you to be with me that you also may be where I am. You know the way to the place where I am going.
John 14: 1-4

Ecclesiastes 7 is a chapter that is highlighted, starred, and underlined in my Bible. It may seem long but far be it from me to slice and dice any part of Scripture. There are parts I don't understand, but I find a lot of wisdom in this Chapter. It is well worth the read.

A good name is better than fine perfume,
And the day of death better than the day of birth.
It is better to go to a house of mourning
Than to go to a house of feasting,
For death is the destiny of every man;
The living should take this to heart.
Sorrow is better than laughter,
Because a sad face is good for the heart.

The heart of the wise is in the house of mourning,
But the heart of fools is in the house of pleasure.
It is better to heed a wise man's rebuke
Than to listen to the song of fools.
Like the crackling of thorns under the pot,
So is the laughter of fools.
This too is meaningless.

Extortion turns a wise man into a fool,
And a bribe corrupts the heart.

The end of a matter is better than its beginning,
And patience is better than pride.
Do not be quickly provoked in your spirit,
For anger resides in the lap of fools.

Do not say, "Why were the old days better than these?"
For it is not wise to ask such questions.

Wisdom, like an inheritance, is a good thing
And benefits those who see the sun.
Wisdom is a shelter
As money is a shelter,
But the advantage of knowledge is this,

That wisdom preserves the life of its possessor.

Consider what God has done:

Who can straighten what he had made crooked?
When times are good, be happy;
But when times are bad, consider;
God has made the one
As well as the other.
Therefore, a man cannot discover anything about his future.

In this meaningless life of mine I have seen both of these:
A righteous man perishing in his righteousness,
And a wicked man living long in his wickedness.

Do not be over righteous,
Neither be over wise -
Why destroy yourself?
Do not be over wicked,
And do not be a fool –
Why die before your time?
It is good to grasp the one
And not let go of the other.
The man who fears God will avoid all extremes.

Wisdom makes one wise man more powerful
than ten rulers in a city.

There is not a righteous man on earth
Who does what is right and never sins

Do not pay attention to every word people say,
Or you may hear your servant cursing you-

For you know in your heart
That many times you yourself
Have cursed others.

All this I tested by wisdom and I said,

"I am determined to be wise" –
But this was beyond me.
Whatever wisdom may be,
It is far off and most profound –
Who can discover it?
So I turned my mind to understand,
To investigate and to search out
Wisdom and the scheme of things
And to understand the stupidity of wickedness
And the madness of folly.

I find more bitter than death
The woman who is a snare,
Whose heart is a trap?
And whose hands are chains.
The man who pleases God will escape her,
But the sinner she will ensnare.

"Look," says the Teacher, "this is what I have discovered:

Adding one thing to another to
Discover the scheme of things –
While I was still searching but not finding –
I found one upright man among a thousand,
But not one upright woman among them all.
This only have I found:

God made mankind upright, but men have gone in search of many schemes."
Ecclesiastes 7

Amen.
Revelations 22:21

Julie Burget Schrock is available for speaking engagements and personal appearances. For more information contact:

Julie Burget Schrock
P.O. Box 160847
Altamonte Springs, FL 32716

missingmax2011@gmail.com

To purchase additional copies of this book or other books published by Advantage Books call our toll free order number at:
1-888-383-3110 (Book Orders Only)

or visit our bookstore website at:
www.advbookstore.com

Advantage BOOKS

Longwood, Florida, USA
"we bring dreams to life"™
www.advbooks.com

CPSIA information can be obtained at www.ICGtesting.com
Printed in the USA
BVOW072031311011

274963BV00001B/1/P

9 781597 552691